BBQ MAKES EVERYTHING BETTER

AARON CHRONISTER AND JASON DAY

SCRIBNER

New York   London   Toronto   Sydney

SCRIBNER
A Division of Simon & Schuster, Inc.
1230 Avenue of the Americas
New York, NY 10020

First Scribner hardcover edition May 2010

SCRIBNER and design are registered trademarks of The Gale Group, Inc.,
used under license by Simon & Schuster, Inc., the publisher of this work.

For information about special discounts for bulk purchases,
please contact Simon & Schuster Special Sales at 1-866-506-1949
or business@simonandschuster.com.

The Simon & Schuster Speakers Bureau can bring authors to your live event.
For more information or to book an event contact the Simon & Schuster Speakers Bureau
at 1-866-248-3049 or visit our website at www.simonspeakers.com.

Manufactured in the United States of America

10   9   8   7   6   5   4   3   2   1

ISBN 978-1-4391-6830-1
ISBN 978-1-4391-6832-5 (ebook)

This book is dedicated to anyone and everyone who's read, cooked, eaten, talked about, forwarded, blogged, tweeted, Digged, Stumbled, bookmarked, or just plain ogled our Bacon Explosion recipe. Without your fascination this wouldn't have been possible, and we sincerely thank you!

Included in this book is a password necessary for accessing the members-only area of the companion website run by the authors. BBQAddicts.com is full of additional recipes and ideas that coincide with the recipes and information included in this book, and a central location to ask questions and interact with both Jason and Aaron on a regular basis. You will be able to contribute to the discussion, upload your own photos or modifications of our recipes, discuss specific equipment and products mentioned in this book, purchase award-winning rubs and sauce, and much more. This invaluable resource comes free with this book and will give you a perfect one-two combination to create mouthwatering BBQ!

CONTENTS

BBQ MAKES EVERYTHING BETTER

INTRODUCTION

Barbecue is a guy thing, a throwback to the spit-roasted woolly mammoth, perhaps. It tends to be written about today (and debated in endless detail) like a sporting event, which in fact it has become: thousands of tiny local competitions are rapidly giving way to several major barbecue leagues, with their own playoffs, World Series—and six-figure purses.

—Molly O'Neill, *American Food Writing*

Back on September 19, 2008, we were just two passionate backyard cooks entering the world of competition barbecue for the first time. We pulled into the parking lot of our first contest not knowing what we were getting ourselves into but confident in the recipes that had pleased our families and friends for years. Twenty-four hours later, as we hoisted cold beers and clasped our awards, we knew our lifelong passion for the backyard grill was officially solidified as a full-fledged addiction.

JASON

Growing up in Kansas City, I've been fully immersed in barbecue culture my entire life. In fact, I can almost pinpoint the exact moment that I was officially bitten by the barbecue bug.

The summer after my junior year of high school, my father arrived home from the office just like any other Friday afternoon. He tossed his briefcase on the kitchen table. A quick flip of the small brass latches and he opened the case to reveal two ziplock bags stuffed full of a dark red powder. He went on to proclaim that a coworker did competition barbecue and had passed along a batch of his super-secret rub and a few of his com-

Pictured from left: Bryant Gish, Aaron Chronister, and Jason Day

petition tricks. Suddenly weekend plans were set as we embarked on our first baby back ribs adventure.

A smoker was still foreign territory in my family. We were strictly gas grillers but certainly enjoyed the fruits of others' labors when it came to barbecue. On this particular weekend, Dad dared to dabble in the smoke. What resulted were the most juicy and tender ribs I had ever eaten. At that exact moment barbecue became a complete and all-consuming experience.

College was the first time I spent an extended amount of time outside of Kansas City. Only two hours down the road at the University of Missouri, barbecue seemed to have dropped off the map. To get my fix, I would host impromptu dorm-room barbecues on my trusty George Foreman grill, cooking up chicken and burgers for anyone who wandered through.

I bought my first smoker while in college, and it didn't take too long for Dad's techniques to start coming back to me. Each smoke session brought back a new memory of his routine. It was only a matter of weeks before the whole neighborhood knew that the faint smell of hickory in the air meant that I was cooking up a feast.

As did so many post-college kids, I moved back in with my folks while I pursued my first "real" job. Thanks to the luxuries of the Internet, job searching only took up a couple hours of my day, which left me plenty of time to obsess over dinner. Soon my daily routine included a trip to the market to pick up ingredients for that night's meal. My mother was probably the biggest fan of my cooking and even extended me an offer to become a permanent house-son. Unfortunately, I quickly found out that single ladies weren't all that impressed with house-sons, so that lifestyle was short-lived. Soon after landing my first job, I met a young lady who recognized and embraced my passion for grilling and barbecue . . . and I married her.

AARON

Growing up in northwest Arkansas, I was sandwiched between Kansas City and Memphis and their distinctly different but equally delicious styles of barbecue. Arkansas barbecue mixed and matched both cities' styles, which gave me a good foundation to eventually become a master of the grill.

Like Jason, I entered the barbecue world when I left home for college. I purchased my first smoker in hopes of making ribs like the ones I ate at Charlie Vergos' Rendezvous in Memphis. Much to my surprise (and chagrin), I found I had no idea what I was doing. Unlike Jason I didn't have any secret rubs or competition tricks to get me started, so I was stuck experimenting. In fact, my first rack of baby back ribs came out tasting like the soot from my chimney and as chewy as a Goodyear tire. My friends and I pretended they were the best things ever, and I'm sure everyone secretly went for pizza when they left.

Not to be deterred, I continued attempting to make the best barbecue I could. Instead of inviting all my friends, I cooked alone, in isolation, while I worked out the kinks. It didn't take long, and pretty soon I was making ribs like the ones in Memphis.

During my time in Arkansas I even invented my own side dish named after yours truly, the Chronion: a cored white onion, stuffed with beef bouillon and butter, seasoned with salt and pepper, and smoked for three hours. Everyone wanted these things like they were Super Bowl tickets. Now someone, somewhere, probably has made this already, but I'm going to go ahead and claim inventor status because I didn't know about it!

Fast-forward five years and I found myself in Kansas City. About two weeks after moving, I stopped to get gas and became confused as to why there was a line of a hundred people out the door. I went in to pay, and the most intoxicating scent I had ever encountered was floating through the air. Little did I know I was standing in the world-famous Oklahoma Joe's Barbecue (yes, it's in a gas station). I paid for my gas, stood in line for an hour or so, and rediscovered my love for barbecue right then and there.

My trip to Oklahoma Joe's that day put me into serious high gear. I went out and bought another smoker and once again started trying to perfect everything I could. This time, however, I was in Kansas City and surrounded by barbecue experts on every corner. My skills improved, and my next goal was competition.

Fast-forward another five years or so (hey, quit trying to figure out how old I am) and I met my wife. All of her friends and the neighborhood discovered how good I am behind the smoker, so every time there is a party (or any other function for that matter), they asked me to cook. Scratch that, they pretty much just inform me that I'm cooking. My soon-to-be-wife mentioned that a college friend of hers had a boyfriend who's into barbecue. We were set up on a man date, and the next thing you know we were cooking for our first competition!

BARBECUE *DOES* MAKE EVERYTHING BETTER

Our worlds came together once our wives first discovered that we shared the same passion for barbecue. We were both interested in starting a competition team, so we partnered with our friend Bryant Gish to create Burnt Finger BBQ. With our first contest only a few short months away, our newly formed team got together for an official practice run. We laid out a time line, did a run-through, and crossed our fingers.

At last, the big day finally arrived. Since this was our first contest, we kicked off the event with a small party to ease any nerves before settling into our competition routine later that evening. As night turned into morning, all of our processes were still on pace with our time lines. As morning became afternoon, each one of our competition meats came off the smoker just as we planned. With only a quick pit stop on the cutting board for final touch-ups, each entry was sent to the judges like clockwork. And as quickly as it began, our first barbecue contest was complete.

While we're always confident in our cooking style, we headed to the awards ceremony with open minds and no real expectations. Little did we know at the time that we'd be walking out of our first barbecue contest with two awards! Fueled by excitement and adrenaline, we decided to enter the American Royal Barbecue.

For those not familiar with the American Royal, it's the world's largest barbecue contest with approximately 500 teams entering the open division every year. It's considered the World Series of barbecue and is THE weekend that makes barbecue teams into barbecue legends. Plus, it's the biggest party Kansas City has to offer with nearly 100,000 people pouring into the festival grounds to embrace barbecue culture.

As with our first contest, we settled into our cooking routine late in the evening and set out to hit our time lines. With the exception of a slight panic attack upon discovering that we overcooked our ribs a bit, everything went smoothly, and we were once again happy with our entries. With fingers crossed, we headed to the awards ceremony hoping our team would crack the top 100.

As the announcer began to cycle through the winners in each category, we eagerly listened, hoping to get a glimpse of some of the legendary barbecue teams that were competing. By the time the brisket category rolled around, we had all lost interest in the awards and were BSing among ourselves. Out of nowhere, we heard a voice from the row behind us say, "Congrats, guys!" As we looked up, we saw the giant projector screen next to the stage displaying "5th Place: Burnt Finger BBQ." Excited and disbelieving, we made our way to the front of the arena to collect our fifth-place brisket ribbon at the biggest barbecue contest in the world.

The American Royal pretty much wrapped up the 2008 season for Burnt Finger BBQ. With the winter cold beginning to set in, we decided to turn our attention to a new project. Since both of us come from a marketing and technology background, we decided to launch a Web site geared toward the barbecue community. Officially launched on October 22, 2008, BBQAddicts.com quickly became our little corner of the Internet.

Not two months after launching the Web site, we received a request from a bacon news group wondering what kind of uses we had for bacon within the barbecue world. We immediately thought of a smoked bacon–wrapped sausage log. In the barbecue community, smoked chubs of sausage are rather common, and are better known as "fatties." Wrapping delicious strips of bacon around a fatty could only make it better, so we set out to document our process for the Web site. After a weekend of cooking, and a "buy-one-get-one-free" special on bacon at the local market, we emerged from our test kitchen with the first Bacon Explosion.

A couple days later we unveiled the recipe to the world through a simple message on Twitter. Bacon Explosion immediately gained a cult following as people began forwarding the recipe to their friends and family. Twitter was instantaneously abuzz with bacon mania, which drove nearly 10,000 unique visitors to our Web site within the first day. Over the next couple of weeks, traffic to the site continued to build. The Bacon Explosion had been sent around the world with strong support on link sites such as StumbleUpon, Digg, and Reddit.

Intrigued by our unique blend of social networking and barbecue expertise, *The New York Times* immediately sent a photographer out to capture the Bacon Explosion in all its glory. At the time of the photo shoot, the *Times* had only informed us that we were in contention for an article. A few days later we received the official call from the editor announcing that our Bacon Explosion was a lock for an article. It wasn't until two short days before the publication hit newsstands we learned that we had actually earned a front-page feature in the January 28 issue of *The New York Times* food section.

Once the article was released, our lives were immediately turned upside down. Our phones were flooded with appearance requests, as our barbecue sausage recipe was garnering attention from major media outlets across the world, including Fox News, CNN, *Kansas City Star,* etc.

The Bacon Explosion has since become a staple recipe for backyard barbecues across the world. We even launched a fully cooked retail version, as well as a line of sauces and rubs, to help amateur cooks achieve the exact flavor of our original Bacon Explosion. Most importantly, though, we're happy to have the chance to share our barbecue passion. This is the food that we love and hope that other backyard grillers will love too. The simple fact is that barbecue really *does* make everything better.

CHAPTER 1

EQUIPMENT, METHODS, AND TECHNIQUES

Give a man a fish and you feed him for a day. Teach a man to fish and you feed him for a lifetime.

—Chinese proverb

Our style of cooking is simple yet effective. It's our mission statement that good food doesn't have to be complicated. But before we get rolling with the recipes, we need to clarify a few terms that we'll be using throughout the book. Barbecue has many interpretations, all of which are completely legitimate, so to avoid any confusion we're fully disclosing the way we'll use these terms in the pages to come.

- **Barbecue**—A method of cooking. A style of cooking. A device for cooking. A party or gathering. A sauce. A blend of spices. Confused yet? To us, barbecue embodies all these things. It's a complete experience that can't be limited to just one cut-and-dried definition.
- **Grilling**—For lots of people, grilling is what they consider to be barbecue. To be more specific though, it's a style of cooking that uses the intense heat of a fire to quickly cook food. This is the most common form of "barbecue" and is generally the technique that is mastered before learning how to smoke.
- **Smoking**—A style of cooking that uses the aromatic smoke and radiant heat of a fire to cook and flavor food. It is generally done using lower temperatures to allow the food to slowly absorb the smoky aroma over a long cooking time. This is the reason why smoking is often referred to as "low and slow" cooking.

Barbecue and smoking have the reputation of being an art that can only be perfected through years of trial and error. While there might be an element of truth to that statement, barbecue is built upon three basic principles. Beyond those, personal preference rules—hence the reason for varied and hotly contested regional styles.

1. **Flavor balance.** A common mistake for the first-time barbecuer is to overwhelm the natural meat flavor with rub, sauce, and/or smoke. The perfect bite of barbecue has all four of these flavors living in complete harmony. The rub, sauce, and smoke should all act as enhancements to the natural flavor of the meat without any one flavor overpowering another.

   The smoky flavor absorbed by the food is a direct result of the type of wood burned during the smoking process. When choosing the type of wood to use, you need to be aware of the flavor that each particular species emits. Keep in mind that flavors are completely subjective, but there are a few woods that can easily overpower the subtle flavor of delicate meats. For example, hickory and mesquite have a much stronger smoke compared to fruity woods such as apple or cherry. Because of this, you will want to pair those woods with a meat that also carries a strong flavor, such as beef. Fish and poultry carry a much lighter flavor, so they should be paired with a subtle smoky flavor. Here's a quick listing of how we choose to pair food with smoke:

   · Beef—Hickory, mesquite, oak, pecan
   · Pork—Apple, cherry, hickory, maple, oak, pecan
   · Poultry—Alder, apple, cherry, maple, oak
   · Fish—Alder, cherry, oak

   Each of these woods is available in a variety of shapes and sizes. Deciding on whether to use pellets, chips, chunks, or logs depends on what type of smoker you are using.

   · Pellets are small pieces of condensed sawdust specifically designed for certain types of grills. Pellet cookers have an electronic hopper system that automatically feeds a fire to generate heat and smoke. Technology has come a long way in the barbecue world, and pellet grills are among the leaders. Some of the newer models have a fully automated control panel similar to an oven. This means that creating a perfectly smoked brisket can be as simple as filling the hopper with pellets and pushing a button. The people that use these types of grills affectionately refer to themselves as "pellet heads."

· Chips are best when you are converting a gas or charcoal grill into a smoker. These types of grills normally don't have a large cooking chamber, so it doesn't take much wood to fill it with smoke. Hardware stores generally carry metal smoker boxes that are designed to slowly burn wood chips. They're rectangular in shape with a removable lid that has holes to allow the smoke to escape. To use the smoker box you simply fill it with wood chips and place it directly on your heat source. To create a homemade smoker box, wrap aluminum foil around a handful of chips and pierce a few holes in the top of the foil with a key or knife.

· Chucks, or two- to three-inch blocks of wood, are best used in medium to large smokers and are what most people utilize when cooking on a dedicated smoker. The wood blocks are laid on top of smoldering coals to generate smoke.

· Logs are used in extremely large smokers. These types of smokers are referred to as "stick burners." The large smoking chamber requires a great amount of heat to keep hot, so charcoal is normally passed over in favor of burning whole logs in a campfire manner.

When discussing fire building and choice of wood, the topic of soaking always comes up. The theory is that by soaking your wood in water you can prevent your wood from catching on fire while also releasing steam into the cooking chamber. Our opinion is that soaking your wood doesn't add any benefit. If you practice good fire-control techniques, you can limit the amount of oxygen that reaches your fire and prevent any flames. This low-oxygen type of environment is primed for a fire to smolder, which is exactly what you need to generate aromatic smoky flavors. We also cook with water pans, so the moisture in the wood is minimal compared to what is released from the steaming pan of water.

2. **Fire control.** This is the single biggest obstacle when first learning to barbecue. Having control over your fire means having the ability to effectively manage the amount of heat applied to your food.

Think of your smoker as an oven. If you were baking a cake, you wouldn't walk over to your oven and turn the temperature gauge up and then ten minutes later turn it way down, would you? The same principle applies to barbecue. A smoker is essentially a wood-fired oven. The smoke is simply an added flavor, just like the rubs or sauces you choose to use. By having your outdoor oven run at a constant temperature, you can more accurately predict your timing and establish a consistent final product each and every time you cook.

The first step to building a controllable fire is to know how much heat it needs to generate. Different recipes call for different temperatures, so you need to be familiar with the various ranges of heat. Here is a quick breakdown of the ranges we'll be referencing:

- High heat = 450 to 650 degrees
- Medium-high heat = 400 to 450 degrees
- Medium heat = 350 to 375 degrees
- Medium-low heat = 300 to 325 degrees
- Low heat = 225 to 275 degrees

Before building a fire, you should understand the choices of fuel that are available. The most common and widely available form of charcoal is the briquette, but our preference is to use all-natural hardwood lump charcoal. The first difference you'll notice when opening a bag of lump charcoal is the appearance. Unlike briquettes, which are all the exact same size and shape, lump charcoal looks like charred pieces of wood. It's made by burning pieces of lumber and wood in an oxygen-deprived environment. The resulting product is an all-natural charcoal that is perfect for barbecuing.

Briquettes are made in the same fashion, but once the initial burn is complete the resulting charcoal is ground up and combined with fillers and additives before compressing. The purpose of these additional ingredients is to improve the performance, but they also have a few undesirable side effects. When first lighting briquettes, there is a distinct odor given off while the coals are ashing over. If you are cooking while this process is taking place, then that odor will impart an undesirable flavor to your food.

Another benefit to hardwood lump charcoal is the amount of ash that is yielded from a burn. One of the added ingredients in briquettes is sand, which helps hold the heat. The downside is that it remains in the bottom of your grill once the fire burns out. You can easily burn three to four times the amount of hardwood lump charcoal before equaling the same amount of ash as one briquette fire.

Now, before we totally write off the use of briquettes, we have to point out that companies are starting to make all-natural hardwood briquettes. They perform the same as hardwood lump charcoal and don't contain the additives of traditional briquettes. You just have to be conscious of the charcoal you're purchasing and make sure you see the words "all-natural hardwood" on the bag.

Now that we've picked out our charcoal, it's time to build the fire. One of the best ways to build a controllable fire is to use a technique called the "Minion Method." Named after its creator, Jim Minion, it's the process of laying down a base of unlit charcoal and placing a few lit pieces of charcoal on top. The unlit pieces are slowly ignited, providing a longer and more efficiently burning fire. To get those few lit pieces we use a device called a charcoal chimney. It's a metal cylinder that's open on both ends with a slotted metal divider inside and a handle on the outside. Charcoal is placed above the metal divider and crumpled newspaper is ignited underneath the divider. The chimney directs the heat and flames of the fire up through the charcoal and efficiently ignites a batch of coals.

To monitor the temperature of your fire, you MUST have some sort of thermometer in your cooker. Just about every commercial grill or smoker comes with a temperature device built in, but these thermometers are normally placed in less-than-ideal locations. To effectively monitor your cooking temperatures, you need to know the temperature where your food is sitting. Lots of manufacturers place the thermometer at the very top of the grill. Since hot air rises, this location tends to be slightly hotter than the actual cooking surface. To counteract this placement error, you can use a basic wired temperature probe skewered through a potato to monitor the temperature of the cooking surface. Slice a medium baking potato in half widthwise and insert the temperature probe all the way through the center parallel to your cut. Place the cut edge of the potato on the grill grate, and you now have a device for monitoring the exact cooking temperature of your food.

Once you have the smoker up to temperature, the next battle is keeping it steady. The easiest way to do this is to adjust the dampers that allow oxygen into the firebox. Closing them cuts off the air supply to the fire, which in turn causes it to cool down. Opening them lets in more oxygen to the fire, which causes it to burn bigger and generate more heat. Now, in the case you get an extreme spike in temperature, or a "flare-up," it's always a good idea to keep a squirt bottle of water nearby, so you can extinguish a small portion of the fire to quickly bring its temperature down.

3. **Meat temperature.** Accurately monitoring the internal temperature of your meat is the absolute easiest way to gauge the degree of doneness. You can take an expensive cut of meat, apply the perfect amount of seasoning, and roast it over a perfectly consistent fire, but if you're unable to recognize the exact moment that it's perfectly cooked, then it all goes to waste.

Ideally you'll want to get to the point of being able to make this determination by the look and feel of the meat, but when starting out, cooking by temperature is a great way to learn how to measure doneness. To accurately monitor internal temperatures, you need to have an accurate piece of equipment by your side. Remember that wired probe that we're using to monitor the temperature of the cooking surface? Those types of devices work great for generally monitoring the internal temperature of your food, but they tend to be inaccurate and/or unreliable for dialing in on that final measure of doneness. If you're serious about cooking perfect barbecue each and every time, then you'll need to step it up a notch. Our overwhelming recommendation for a temperature monitoring device is the Thermapen. It's a highly accurate instant-read thermometer with a waterproof casing.

WHAT YOU NEED TO SMOKE

While there are plenty of commercial smokers that are specifically designed to make smoking food easier, it's not required that you own one of these devices. With a few slight adjustments you can turn a basic grill that you already own into a makeshift smoker.

The main principle for turning a grill into a smoker is to establish an indirect heat source. This is accomplished by moving the food away from the fire or by placing an object (generally a water pan) between the food and fire. This process allows only the gentle radiant heat to reach the food so that it can cook slowly.

Converting a Gas Grill to a Smoker

The most common piece of barbecue equipment owned is the standard gas grill. Turning this style of grill into a smoker depends on what type of grill you own.

- **Two-burner grill**—Turn off one of the burners and place your food on the opposite side of the grill from your heat source. Place wood chips directly above the hot burner in a foil packet or smoker box.
- **Three-burner grill**—Turn off the middle burner and place your food in the center of the grill. Place wood chips directly above one of the hot burners in a foil packet or smoker box.
- **Dual-rack grill**—Turn on all burners and place a pan of water on the lower grate above the fire. Disposable aluminum pans found at the grocery store work best for this. Place your food on the upper rack of the grill so that it is suspended over the top of the water pan. Place wood chips next to the water pan directly above the hot burners in a foil packet or smoker box.

No matter what type of grill you have, you need to keep the lid closed while cooking to keep the heat trapped inside. Just remember, "If you're looking, you ain't cooking."

Converting a Charcoal Grill to a Smoker

The second most common piece of equipment is the charcoal grill. To convert this style of grill to a smoker, you just need to pile your lit coals on one of the far sides of the grill and place your food on the opposite side. Wood chunks can be placed directly on the hot coals to create the aromatic smoke. As with the gas grill, you need to keep the lid closed while cooking to keep the heat trapped inside.

COMMONLY ASKED QUESTIONS

How Long Does It Take to Cook?

A common question asked by newcomers to the barbecue world is "How long will it take to cook my ____?" The correct answer to this question is that there is no set time. When grilling over high heat, the time variance isn't as apparent because of the quick cook times, but slow smoking a large piece of meat over an extended period of time easily exposes the variance of each cut. As we explained earlier, each cook should be working toward testing for doneness through look and touch, but for now these general guidelines will get you started:

- Brisket: 1 to 1½ hours per pound: 200 degrees internal
- Beef ribs: 1½ to 2 hours per pound: 200 degrees internal
- Pork shoulder: 1 to 1½ hours per pound: 200 degrees internal
- Pork ribs: 1½ to 2 hours per pound: 200 degrees internal
- Whole chicken: 45 to 60 minutes per pound: 165 degrees internal
- Whole turkey: 30 to 45 minutes per pound: 165 degrees internal

Should the Fat Side Be Up or Down?

When cooking large cuts of meat such as pork butts and briskets, there is always one side that is covered by a thick layer of fat known as the fat cap. The question as to which direction to face the fat cap during the cooking process has been debated countless times, and there are plenty of theories to defend either approach. We believe that both methods can be correct, depending on what type of smoker you use. Instead of arbitrarily picking a direction, you should closely examine how the heat source will reach the meat during the cooking process. The direction that works best for your cooker will be the one that puts the fat cap between the most intense heat and the meat. The fat will act as insulation to shield the meat from the harsh heat. Vertical and recessed side smokers deliver heat from the bottom, so you'll want to cook with the fat cap down. Convection-style cookers are designed to pull the hot smoke across the top of the meat, so for these you'll want to have the fat cap facing up.

Why Does the Internal Meat Temperature Stop Rising During My Cook?

When cooking pork butt or brisket, it's common for the internal temperature of the meat to plateau somewhere in the neighborhood of 160 and 170 degrees. In fact, it's not uncommon for the temperature to even drop a few degrees when it reaches this point. This can occur for upward of two hours while the energy from the heat source is being used to convert collagen into gelatin. Collagen is part of the tough connective tissue that holds muscles together. Stronger muscles contain a higher percentage of this connective tissue, which can cause them to be tough and chewy when cooked improperly. But when cooked slowly at low temperatures, the collagen is converted into a rich gelatin that gives barbecue its delicious flavor. When the plateau occurs, it's best to continue cooking just as you were before the temperature halted. Eventually it will break through the plateau, and the temperature will begin to rise again.

How Can I Check the Airflow of My Grill/Smoker?

The main principle for establishing good airflow is to have an intake location near your fire and an output location that draws the hot air from the fire across your food. In a traditional charcoal grill this is accomplished by having adjustable vents in the bottom of the charcoal pan, which allows the air to flow into the burning charcoal. The food is then suspended directly above the hot charcoal on a metal grate with the output vent directly above the food (typically on the lid of the grill). You can control the airflow of your grill by adjusting these vents: opening and closing the intake vents lets you control how hot your fire burns; opening and closing the output vents lets you control how much heat is trapped within the cooking chamber.

THE HOLY TRINITY OF BARBECUE: RIBS, PORK SHOULDER, AND BRISKET

The three cuts of meat that define barbecue are pork ribs, pork shoulder, and beef brisket. They're also the three cuts that have the most regional variance across the country. To get you started down the barbecue path, we're going to give you the ins and outs of the Holy Trinity of Barbecue.

Pork Ribs

Ribs come from one of two cuts: the side (spareribs) or the back (baby back ribs) of a hog. Spareribs are a large meaty cut that contain a fair amount of fat. They're also a less tender cut compared to the baby back rib, which accounts for the longer cooking time. Baby back ribs are a smaller, leaner, less meaty cut but tend to be higher in price.

When picking spareribs, you'll find that they are available in two ways: whole and St. Louis style. St. Louis–style spareribs are simply trimmed slabs of whole spareribs. If you're short on time and aren't able to trim them yourself, then pretrimmed St. Louis–style ribs are the way to go, just be conscious that you pay more for the trimmed variety. If you have the time, we recom-

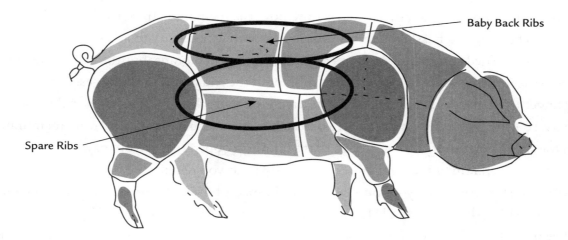

Baby Back Ribs

Spare Ribs

mend that you buy whole slabs and trim them yourself. Not only is it more cost effective but also you have control over where the cuts are made, and plus you can cook all the trimmings for a snack or to flavor your beans.

To trim a whole slab of spareribs into St. Louis–style spareribs, you first need to understand what portions need to be removed. There are four main portions to pay attention to: the ribs, the sternum, the cartilage, and the skirt.

The concept behind St. Louis–style spareribs is to remove the sternum, cartilage, and skirt, leaving only the rectangular slab of ribs. To do this, first lay the slab with the bone side facing upward. There will be a loose flap of meat that runs across the slab. This is called the skirt and needs to be removed. To do so, run a sharp knife along the base of the skirt, trimming as close to the slab as possible.

At the top of the slab there is a large bony portion, which is the sternum. To remove this bony portion you will need to cut through the cartilage that connects the sternum to the ribs. To locate this area, hold the sternum with one hand and the ribs with the other. Slowly bend the center section upward, and you should see where the slab bends. Using a sharp knife, cut through this area and separate the sternum from the slab. If done correctly, you should now have an evenly trimmed slab of ribs. Chop off the loose ends to create a perfect rectangle. Keep in mind that baby back ribs come from a different area of the hog, so they don't require this step. Some people prefer to remove the loin strap (a long strip of meat running across the front of the slab), but in general removing excess fat is the only trimming that you'll need to do.

After trimming, the next crucial step is to remove the membrane from the bone side of the slab. It can be a bit of a hassle to remove, but it's absolutely necessary to achieve a tender final product. We've tried many different ways of removing the membrane, but the easiest and simplest is to use a butter knife to loosen the membrane at the end of one of the bones. Gently work your finger underneath the loosened edge to create small pocket. The raw meat will be rather slippery, so use a paper towel to get a grip on the loosened edge and pull the entire membrane from the slab. Sometimes you'll get a slab that's not very cooperative, so you may have to repeat this process several times if the membrane breaks apart as you're removing it. If you have trouble with this step, try asking your butcher for preskinned ribs. They may not have any on hand, but if you're nice, they're normally happy to remove the membrane for you.

The other tip to keep in mind is that no matter what anyone tells you, never ever boil your ribs. While this is an easy way to cook ribs, it ends up boiling out the flavor. Unless your sole intention is to make pork stock, your ribs should never be anywhere near a pot of boiling water.

Ribs are a great example of the variance in barbecue cooking times because they come in many different shapes, sizes, and thicknesses. Although general guidelines like the 3-2-1 Method will get you in the ballpark, only experience and feel will get you to your exact seats.

There are a few different theories for checking doneness on ribs. We use the simple "Bend Test." Using a pair of tongs, pick up the slab of ribs and examine the surface of the meat where the slab bends. This is typically just beyond where your tongs grip the slab. If the fibers of meat begin breaking apart, then the slab is done. If the slab is still rather tough and holds together, then it needs to be returned to the cooker. If the slab completely falls apart and the bones fall out, then the slab is actually overdone. No need to worry, though. Overdone ribs can be quite delicious as long as they haven't gotten to the point of drying out. When cooking at home, we actually prefer our ribs to be slightly overcooked, though this is a big no-no when cooking in competitions.

(NOTE: The 3-2-1 Method is a common guideline used to cook ribs. It stands for 3 hours of smoke, 2 hours wrapped in foil, and 1 hour of additional smoke.)

SIMPLE BARBECUED PORK RIBS

INGREDIENTS

1 slab St. Louis–style
 pork ribs
2 tablespoons yellow
 mustard
Any commercial pork rub
1 tablespoon apple juice
Simple Kansas City–Style
 Sauce (page 37)

EQUIPMENT

Sharp knife
Smoker
Apple wood
Heavy-duty aluminum foil

Ribs tend to be the first cut of meat that people reach for when purchasing a smoker. Although they can be relatively easy to cook, they don't take too well to an uncontrolled smoker. Our advice is to practice fire control using a pork butt (page 25), then move on to this recipe once you've mastered the art of hovering at 225 degrees.

STEP 1: Trim away any remaining loose fat from the ribs and slather the ribs with the yellow mustard.

STEP 2: Thoroughly coat the ribs with your favorite pork rub to create a paste with the mustard. Massage the mixture into the meat.

STEP 3: Smoke with apple wood over indirect heat at 225 degrees.

STEP 4: After 3 hours (2 hours for back ribs), double wrap the slab in heavy-duty aluminum foil with the apple juice and return to the smoker.

STEP 5: After 2 hours, open the foil packets and use the bend test (page 20) to check for doneness. If the slab is done to your liking, glaze it with barbecue sauce and return it to the smoker for another

15 minutes to set the sauce. If the slab is not quite done, return it to the smoker for another 30 minutes to continue cooking. Repeat this process until the ribs are done to your liking.

STEP 6: Remove the ribs from the smoker, slice, and serve.

Note: Pair Simple Barbecued Pork Ribs with Simple Kansas City—Style Sauce (page 37).

Pork Shoulder

The general concept of creating a delicious pulled pork sandwich is to slow smoke a tough cut of pork to render the fatty connective tissue, leaving meat that is so juicy and tender that it can be "pulled" apart. The long cooking time allows the large shoulder to soak up a tremendous amount of smoky flavor, making it one of the flagship barbecue dishes.

Although certain portions of the country prefer to roast a whole hog for their pulled pork, we prefer sticking with the cuts that come from the shoulder section. The most common cut among competition cookers is the Boston butt.

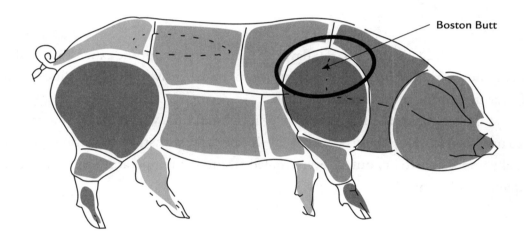

Boston Butt

Now we know what you're thinking when you hear the name, but the Boston butt is actually taken from the shoulder blade area of the front leg of a hog. Its name dates back to colonial times when the less desirable cuts of pork (like the front legs) were stored in large casks known as "butts" for preservation and transportation. The Boston area had a unique and popular way of butchering the top shoulder portion, which is what we know today as the Boston butt.

The second shoulder cut used to create pulled pork is called the "picnic." This cut sits directly below the Boston butt and contains the leg bone. The meat itself is closer in texture and flavor to uncured ham, which isn't surprising seeing as ham is cut from the same location on the rear legs of the hog. We've yet to find concrete evidence as to where this cut gets its name,

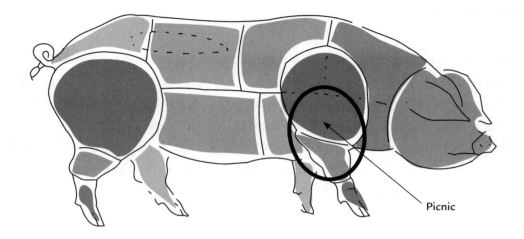

Picnic

but it's said that since it's so similar in flavor to ham (but without the expense), people used to consider it more of a lunchtime meat as opposed to the expensive dinner cut. Since picnics were all the rage in colonial times, the name stuck.

Pork shoulder contains a large amount of fatty marbling, which makes it a perfect cut of meat to use when learning the art of barbecue. It can easily withstand higher temperatures and is virtually impossible to dry out, so even a failed attempt at temperature control will still yield a completely edible meal.

SIMPLE BARBECUED PULLED PORK

INGREDIENTS

1 5-pound pork butt

2 tablespoons yellow
    mustard

Any commercial pork rub

¼ cup apple juice

½ cup Simple Carolina-
    Style Vinegar Sauce
    (page 38)

EQUIPMENT

Smoker

Apple wood

Heavy-duty aluminum foil

2 forks

Although quite simple to prepare, a good pork shoulder will take a fair amount of time and patience to perfect. The cuts are rather hefty and contain a high percentage of fat and connective tissue, so lengthy cooking times are needed to fully tenderize the meat.

STEP 1: Trim any loose fat from the pork butt and slather the meat with the yellow mustard.

STEP 2: Thoroughly coat the pork butt with your favorite pork rub to create a paste with the mustard. Massage the mixture into the meat.

STEP 3: Place the pork butt in the smoker and smoke with apple wood over indirect heat at 225 degrees.

STEP 4: Once the internal temperature reaches 160 degrees, double wrap the pork in heavy-duty aluminum foil with the apple juice and return to the smoker.

STEP 5: Once the internal temperature reaches 200 degrees, remove the foil-wrapped butt from the smoker and let rest for 30 minutes.

STEP 6: Using 2 forks, completely shred the pork butt and discard any excess fat.

STEP 7: Combine ½ cup of the drippings from the foil with the barbecue sauce and pour over the shredded pork.

STEP 8: Serve on potato rolls.

Note: Pair Simple Barbecued Pulled Pork with Simple Carolina-Style Vinegar Sauce (page 38) or Simple Mustard-Style Sauce (page 39).

Beef Brisket

When somebody mentions smoked beef, we automatically think of brisket. It's the Cadillac of the barbecue world and considered to be the most difficult of the classic barbecue meats. When improperly cooked, brisket can be dry, chewy, and as tough as leather, but when handled with care, it can be the most tender, juicy, and flavorful cut of meat you'll ever taste.

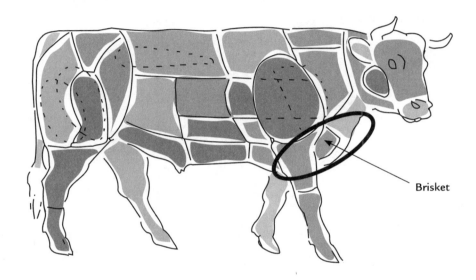

Brisket

A whole untrimmed brisket (also known as packer-cut brisket) contains two separate and distinctive muscles, the point and the flat. The point is the large fatty cut that sits at the far end of the brisket, while the flat is the long rectangular portion that runs the length of the cut. While equally delicious, each cut cooks up differently and requires its own unique serving method. The flat is sliced thinly across the grain, while the point is cut into cubes and returned to the smoker in a sauce bath to create those delicious burnt ends that we all love.

The main reason a brisket can be so difficult to cook is because of the large amount of connective tissue found within the meat. The cut is a heavily used muscle found on the front of the chest near the sternum. Each animal yields two briskets, one from each side of beef. Barbecue folklore has it that "left-handed" briskets are more tender than their "right-handed" counterparts. The theory is that cattle generally lie on their left sides, which causes the muscles on the right side to be used when the animal stands back up. The strengthened muscle means more connective tissue and less fatty marbling, which translates into a tougher/drier cut of meat.

Although this theory earns brownie points for creativity, we've yet to recognize its validity. Many times we've cooked left- and right-handed briskets side by side without any noticeable differences. To tell which side your brisket comes from, hold it in front of you grasping the flat with the point facing downward and the fat cap facing away from you. Now take a glance at the point and check to see which way it curves. If it's pointing to your left side, then it's a left-handed brisket (and vice versa).

SIMPLE BARBECUED BRISKET

INGREDIENTS

1 7-pound whole
    untrimmed brisket
2 tablespoons yellow
    mustard
Any commercial beef rub
¼ cup beef broth
Simple Texas-Style Sauce
    (page 40)

EQUIPMENT

Smoker
Cherry wood
Heavy-duty aluminum foil
Slicing knife
Aluminum pan

Once you know the ropes, a tender brisket is quite easy to prepare. It's all about maintaining a constant heat in your smoker and keeping a close eye on the internal temperature of the beef. Although the cooking times are long, it's well worth the wait, and the leftovers serve as a great base for chili (page 145).

STEP 1: Trim any loose fat from the brisket and slather the meat with the yellow mustard.

STEP 2: Thoroughly coat the brisket with your favorite beef rub to create a paste with the mustard. Massage the mixture into the meat.

STEP 3: Place the brisket in the smoker and smoke with cherry wood over indirect heat at 225 degrees.

STEP 4: Once the internal temperature reaches 160 degrees, double wrap the brisket in heavy-duty aluminum foil with the beef broth and return to the smoker.

STEP 5: Once the internal temperature reaches 200 degrees, remove the foil-covered brisket from the smoker and let rest for 30 minutes.

STEP 6: Using a large sharp knife, separate the point from the flat by slicing through the fat seam that holds the two cuts of meat together. The seam will be rather easy to identify once cooked, and your knife should easily glide through the gelatinous fat. Remove any excess fat from both the point and the flat to leave only the beautifully smoked beef.

STEP 7: Cut the point portion of the brisket into 1-inch cubes (to create burnt ends) and cover with barbecue sauce in an aluminum pan. Smoke the cubes for 30 to 60 minutes longer until the fat is rendered and the sauce caramelizes.

STEP 8: Slice the flat into thin strips and serve on hamburger buns.

Note: Pair Simple Barbecued Brisket with Simple Texas-Style Sauce (page 40).

THE UGLY STEPCHILD OF BARBECUE—CHICKEN

We should start by saying that we're big fans of barbecue chicken, but for one reason or another, this protein gets a bad rap from competition cookers. It's one of the four KCBS categories, and is required if you want to be in contention for a grand championship. But that doesn't stop many of the pitmasters from voicing their frustrations with this category.

A common concern is that cooks are allowed to turn in any part of the chicken they choose, in sharp contrast to the other three categories (ribs, pork, and brisket) that strictly define which cut of meat can be used. The other grumble is that cooking chicken doesn't take as much skill as the other categories, so it's perceived that any Joe Six-Pack can win the category. We don't necessarily view that as a bad thing, though.

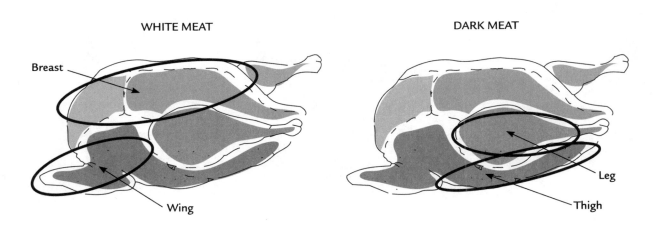

WHITE MEAT

Breast

Wing

DARK MEAT

Leg

Thigh

Poultry is typically butchered into four standard cuts of meat: legs, thighs, breasts, and wings. For chicken, these cuts are then categorized a step further as either white meat (breasts and wings) or dark meat (legs and thighs). The simple explanation for why animals have white and dark meat is that they use each of their muscles differently. The detailed explanation is that dark meat gets its coloring from a higher content of myoglobin proteins, which are responsible for delivering oxygen to muscles. Since oxygen is vital to muscle movement, it's only natural that the most-used muscles have more of these proteins. In chickens, a mostly nonflying bird, the legs and thighs are comprised of dark meat, while the less-used wings and breasts are made up of white meat. A duck, on the other hand, is an avid flier, so most of its body is made up of dark meat.

The cut of chicken overwhelmingly used in competition is the thigh. Since thighs are dark meat, they have a higher fat content than the other cuts, which adds flavor and keeps the meat from drying out. It's also one of the thicker cuts on a chicken, so the meat is able to retain more heat while your entry is patiently waiting to be sampled by the judges. We wouldn't want them tasting our prize recipes cold, would we?

SIMPLE BARBECUED CHICKEN

INGREDIENTS

6 chicken thighs

1 cup zesty Italian dressing

2 tablespoons barbecue rub

1 cup Simple Kansas City–Style Sauce (page 37)

1 cup honey

EQUIPMENT

Smoker

Apple wood

Gallon-sized ziplock bag

Small aluminum pan

Aluminum foil

One of the characteristics associated with barbecue chicken is thick, rubbery skin. This occurs because the low-and-slow cooking style doesn't generate enough heat to render the fat in the skin before the meat is cooked. For most people this is unappetizing, and will more than likely result in the skin being pulled off and thrown in the trash. To remedy this situation, we wrap our chicken in aluminum foil during cooking in the same manner as a pork butt, brisket, or ribs. The foil wrapping encases the chicken in steam, which creates a roasting effect. If done correctly, you'll have chicken that's fall-off-the-bone tender.

STEP 1: Trim any loose fat or extra skin from the chicken thighs.

STEP 2: Place the chicken thighs in a gallon-sized ziplock bag and add the dressing. Turn the chicken thighs so that each piece is evenly coated with dressing. Squeeze any excess air out of the bag, seal, and refrigerate for 2 to 4 hours, turning over halfway through.

STEP 3: Remove the chicken thighs from the marinade and place on a work surface. Wipe away any excess dressing remaining on the chicken thighs and discard the ziplock bag. Evenly coat each chicken thigh with your favorite barbecue rub.

STEP 4: Place the chicken thighs into a 225-degree smoker over indirect heat for 1 hour. While the chicken is smoking, combine the barbecue sauce and honey in a small aluminum pan.

STEP 5: Remove the chicken thighs from the smoker and place in the pan with the barbecue sauce and honey mixture. Cover the pan with a piece of aluminum foil, tightly sealing the edges.

STEP 6: Place the pan back into the 225-degree smoker over indirect heat until the internal temperature of the thighs reaches 185 degrees, approximately 2 to 3 hours.

STEP 7: Remove the pan from the smoker. Before serving, glaze the chicken thighs with the drippings from the pan.

White and dark chicken meat contain different levels of fat, so each has a different ideal temperature for doneness. Dark meat is best at an internal temperature of 185 degrees, while white meat will begin to dry out if taken higher than 165 degrees. If you choose to substitute white meat in this recipe, just reduce the amount of time spent in the foil wrap by approximately 1 hour.

Note: Pair Simple Barbecued Chicken with Simple Kansas City–Style Sauce (page 37).

THE SCHOOL OF SAUCE

The regional variations of barbecue are most evident in the sauces that adorn the smoked meat of the area. Among the most recognized is the thick Kansas City–style barbecue sauce. Known for its deep-red color and sweet molasses flavor, it's the most common style among commercial sauces (KC Masterpiece, Bull's-Eye, Sweet Baby Ray's, etc.), but that doesn't mean it's the only type of sauce out there.

If you head to the Carolina area, you'll quickly find out that molasses, or even tomato, has no place in their style of barbecue. This part of the country is known for its affinity for swine, so people there have come to love vinegar-based sauces that complement the rich flavor of pork.

In North Carolina, a thin and spicy vinegar sauce reigns supreme. The big bold tang of the vinegar dominates the flavor, but it's the blend of peppers that leaves a delightful burn on your lips after each bite. This region also sports a toned-down version called a Piedmont sauce that incorporates tomatoes to mellow out some of the vinegar flavor.

Heading into South Carolina, you can find a mustard-based sauce that's said to be inspired by the German population that originally settled in this area. Honey and peppers typically round out the heavy mustard flavor to create a balanced sauce to use on pulled pork topped with zesty coleslaw.

Texas-style sauce is a semithick tomato-based sauce typically flavored with ingredients similar to those used in the familiar Tex-Mex cuisine of the area. Cumin, chiles, and peppers play into a bold sauce that's designed to stand up against the strong flavor of Texas beef.

Regardless of which style you prefer, barbecue sauce is intended to complement the flavor of the meat. Use it sparingly, but use it often!

If you would like to make your own barbecue sauce for any of the recipes, use the following homemade recipes on pages 37 to 40 in place of the barbecue sauce called for. For example, any recipe that calls for a Kansas City–style barbecue sauce will work with our own Simple Kansas City–Style Sauce. The same holds for our Simple Carolina-Style Vinegar Sauce (any vinegar-based barbecue sauce) or Simple Mustard-Style Sauce (any mustard-based sauce). If you would prefer to buy a sauce but cannot find one, visit our website at http://www.bbqaddicts.com/rubs-sauces/ to experiment with a selection of championship-winning bottled sauces and rubs.

For the basic ribs, pork, brisket, and chicken recipes that appear on pages 21 to 33, pair with the sauces as follows:

Simple Barbecued Pork Ribs with Simple Kansas City—Style Sauce

Simple Barbecued Pulled Pork with Simple Carolina-Style Vinegar Sauce or Simple Mustard-Style Sauce

Simple Barbecued Brisket with Simple Texas-Style Sauce

Simple Barbecued Chicken with Simple Kansas City—Style Sauce

SIMPLE KANSAS CITY–STYLE SAUCE

Yield Approximately 2 cups

This sauce is a classic Kansas City–style barbecue sauce. Its thick texture makes it great for glazing ribs and chicken, yet the flavor is mild enough to not overpower the meat.

STEP 1: Mix all ingredients together in a medium saucepan over medium heat, stirring frequently.

STEP 2: As soon as the sauce begins to boil, reduce the heat to low and simmer for 20 minutes. Continue stirring the sauce frequently to prevent scorching.

INGREDIENTS

1 cup ketchup

½ cup brown sugar

¼ cup red wine vinegar

2 tablespoons molasses

2 tablespoons dark corn syrup

½ tablespoon butter

½ teaspoon liquid smoke

¼ teaspoon kosher salt

¼ teaspoon coarse black pepper

¼ teaspoon paprika

⅛ teaspoon chili powder

⅛ teaspoon garlic granules

⅛ teaspoon minced onions

⅛ teaspoon cayenne pepper

EQUIPMENT

Medium saucepan

Spatula

SIMPLE CAROLINA-STYLE VINEGAR SAUCE

½ cup apple cider

1 tablespoon brown
   sugar

1½ cups white vinegar

1 tablespoon paprika

1 tablespoon cayenne
   pepper

1 teaspoon kosher salt

1 teaspoon coarse black
   pepper

EQUIPMENT

Medium saucepan

Spatula

Yield Approximately 2 cups

Splash a few spoonfuls of this sauce on a pulled pork sandwich for a tangy meal that will leave your lips tingling.

STEP 1: Mix together the apple cider and brown sugar in a medium saucepan over medium heat, stirring frequently until the brown sugar has completely dissolved.

STEP 2: Remove from heat and stir in the remaining ingredients.

If the vinegar flavor is too strong for your tastes, convert this recipe to a Piedmont sauce by adding ½ cup of ketchup.

SIMPLE MUSTARD-STYLE SAUCE

Yield Approximately 2 cups

INGREDIENTS

1 cup yellow mustard

¼ cup honey

¼ cup brown sugar

¼ cup white vinegar

½ teaspoon coarse black
    pepper

¼ teaspoon onion
    powder

¼ teaspoon cayenne
    pepper

EQUIPMENT

Medium saucepan
Spatula

Mustard-style sauces are another product of the Carolinas, which means they were invented for pork. This particular sauce has a hint of sweetness paired with a bold tangy mustard flavor and a touch of heat.

STEP 1: Mix all ingredients together in a medium saucepan over medium heat, stirring frequently.

STEP 2: As soon as the sauce begins to boil, reduce the heat to low and simmer for 5 to 10 minutes. Continue stirring the sauce frequently to prevent scorching.

SIMPLE TEXAS-STYLE SAUCE

INGREDIENTS

1½ cups tomato sauce

½ cup beef stock

½ cup white vinegar

¼ cup sugar

1 tablespoon
    Worcestershire sauce

1 tablespoon chili
    powder

1 tablespoon butter

1 teaspoon cumin

1 teaspoon cayenne
    pepper

EQUIPMENT

Medium saucepan

Spatula

Yield Approximately 2 cups

Bold flavor designed for a bold meat. Texas likes everything bigger, including their flavor.

STEP 1: Mix all ingredients together in a medium saucepan over medium heat, stirring frequently.

STEP 2: As soon as the sauce begins to boil, reduce the heat to low and simmer for 5 to 10 minutes. Continue stirring the sauce frequently to prevent scorching.

CHAPTER 2

BACON

I enjoy having breakfast in bed. I like waking up to the smell of bacon, sue me. And since I don't have a butler, I have to do it myself. So, most nights before I go to bed, I will lay six strips of bacon out on my George Foreman grill. Then I go to sleep. When I wake up, I plug in the grill. I go back to sleep again. Then I wake up to the smell of crackling bacon. It is delicious, it's good for me, it's the perfect way to start the day.

—Michael Scott, *The Office*

When classifying the general population, it's safe to assume that most everyone fits into one of two basic categories: Bacon People or Chocolate People. We're sure there's a few "both" people floating around out there, but for the sake of simplicity we're reducing this classification to the old-fashioned "if you were stuck on an island and could only have one" scenario. For centuries Chocolate People have reigned supreme. Their sweet delicacy is found on every restaurant's menu, and in most cases it's offered up in multiple forms. If chocolate ice cream isn't your style, you can always spring for a warm slice of chocolate cake. What's that . . . cake doesn't satisfy your choco-urges? How about a fudge brownie that's been braised in chocolate syrup, dredged with mini chocolate chips, and topped with chocolate mousse whipped cream? Okay, so maybe that last one doesn't exist, but you get the point. Chocolate People have had their time in the limelight, but the time has come for Bacon People to rise up.

It goes without saying that we're Bacon People. Bacon is quite possibly the most perfect food known to man (or as we put it, "meat candy"). Borne of necessity before the luxury of modern refrigeration, cured strips of pork belly are a perfectly balanced combination of salt, sugar, and fat. Toss in some classic barbecue flavor, and you've got a delicacy worth fasting for . . . although good luck trying to talk us into skipping a meal!

In this chapter you'll find some of our favorite ways to barbecue bacon. Some are original recipes, others are a new take on a classic, and we've even tossed in a favorite from a good friend. But before you indulge in a bacon feast, we want to pass along a piece of advice that was given to us at the Blue Ribbon Bacon Festival in Des Moines: "Don't forget to take off your rings!!!"

BACON EXPLOSION

Yield 10 to 12 servings

The Bacon Explosion is hands down our flagship recipe. It's been sent around the world on the Internet and has been hailed by some as the most downloaded recipe of all time. An ever-growing cult following has popped up in the form of a Facebook fan page (www .facebook.com/BaconExplosion), and we have even been cited as the inspiration behind Web sites such as ThisIsWhyYoureFat.com and BaconJew.com. Since this is the recipe that catapulted us into pop culture fame, it seems only fitting that we honor the recipe that started it all. Behold . . . the BACON EXPLOSION!!!

INGREDIENTS

2 pounds thick-cut bacon

2 tablespoons Burnt Finger BBQ Rub or your favorite rub, divided

2 pounds bulk Italian sausage

1 cup Burnt Finger BBQ Sauce or sweet Kansas City–style barbecue sauce, divided

EQUIPMENT

Smoker

Hickory wood

Gallon-sized ziplock bag

Scissors

Skillet

Brush

STEP 1: To kick off the construction of this pork medley, you'll need to create a bacon basket weave using approximately 1 pound of raw bacon. The number of strips used in the weave will depend on the size and type of bacon you choose to use. Oscar Mayer's Hearty Thick Cut Bacon comes out to be a 5 x 5-inch bacon weave every time, but depending on the brand you choose, you may have to include a few more slices to create an even bacon weave. To create the weave, place 5 strips of bacon side by side. Next, fold back the second and fourth strips and lay another strip of bacon perpendicular to the first layer across the first, third, and fifth strips. Unfold the second and fourth strips back to their original position to create an over/under pattern. Next, fold back the first, third, and fifth strips and place another slice of bacon perpendicular to the first layer across the second and fourth strips. Unfold the first, third, and fifth strips to their original position. Take note of the alternating pattern that has been created. Repeat this process for the rest of the weave.

STEP 2: The next step is to add a layer of barbecue seasoning on top of the bacon weave. Our original recipe calls for 1 tablespoon of Burnt Finger BBQ's pork rub, but you can substitute any sweet or hot rub you'd like.

Just make sure to use a rub that's not overly salty. Bacon already contains a hefty dose of salt, so it's rather easy to overseason with a sodium-heavy rub. Most grocery stores carry rubs labeled "sweet," but the best way to test the salt content is to taste the rub. If salt dominates the flavor, then you should look for a different rub or sweeten it by combining 1 teaspoon brown sugar with 2 teaspoons rub. Once you have your rub picked out (or doctored), evenly sprinkle 1 tablespoon across the bacon weave.

STEP 3: Now that the bacon is well seasoned, it's time to add a layer of sausage. Although pressing out a patty by hand works just fine, the easiest method for creating the sausage layer is to place the bulk Italian sausage inside a gallon-sized ziplock bag. Evenly press the sausage to the edges of the bag to create a uniform patty. Remove the sausage from the bag by using scissors or a knife to cut along both side edges of the bag. Gently remove the sausage patty, keeping it intact, and place it on top of the bacon weave. If there is more than ½ inch of bacon showing around the edges of the sausage layer, expand the sausage layer by pressing the edges outward. Ideally, the sausage layer should be approximately ½ inch thick to create the pinwheel effect seen in the final product.

STEP 4: In a skillet, fry the remaining strips of bacon to your liking. This should be roughly 1 pound of raw bacon, but it could be more or less depending on how much was used in the bacon weave. If you like soft bacon, make it soft. If you like crunchy bacon, make it crunchy. If you like your bacon burnt to hell so the smoke detectors go off, then burn it to hell so the smoke detectors go off. These fried strips are going to be a major part of the inner flavor of the Bacon Explosion, so cook them your favorite way. Regardless of how well done you like yours, you'll need to crumble or chop the cooked strips into bite-sized pieces and place them on top of the sausage layer. (Note: It's okay, and encouraged, to snack on these pieces while you're chopping/crumbling. Just keep in mind that once those cooked bacon morsels touch the raw sausage, you'll need to resist all temptation to nibble. Raw meat can carry food-borne illness, so we definitely want to cook the pork to a safe temperature before indulging. This bit of self-restraint can and will be difficult, but hospital trips are no fun, so stay strong.)

STEP 5: Since this is a barbecue recipe, we need to add another layer of barbecue flavor. Drizzle ½ cup Burnt Finger BBQ sauce all over the top of the cooked bacon pieces. Just like the rub, this is an ingredient that can

be chosen according to personal preference. While the Burnt Finger BBQ products are the official flavors of the Bacon Explosion, any locally available sauce will work just as well.

STEP 6: Now comes the fun part. Carefully separate the back edge of the sausage layer from the bacon weave and begin rolling toward you. You want to include all layers EXCEPT the bacon weave in your roll. Try to keep the sausage as tight as possible and be sure to release any air pockets that form. Once the sausage is fully rolled up, pinch together the seam and ends to seal all the bacon goodness inside. This will also prevent the barbecue sauce from oozing out as it cooks.

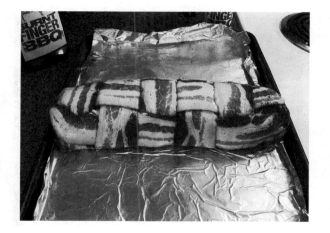

STEP 7: At this point you can start to see the final shape of the Bacon Explosion, but we're missing one key item. To complete the construction process, roll the sausage log forward, completely wrapping it in the bacon weave. Make sure it sits with the seam facing down so that the weight of the sausage roll will keep the bacon weave in place.

STEP 8: Sprinkle 1 tablespoon Burnt Finger BBQ pork rub on the outside of the bacon weave, and now this bad boy is ready for the cooker. Smoke your Bacon Explosion over indirect heat at 225 degrees until the inter-

nal temperature reaches 165 degrees. Normally this will take about 1 hour for each inch of thickness, but that can vary depending on how well you maintain your fire and how many times you open the smoker to take a peek.

STEP 9: Once the Bacon Explosion is fully cooked, we need to add some finishing flavors. Remember the Burnt Finger BBQ sauce that we used for inner flavor? We'll be using that same sauce to glaze the cooked bacon weave. Using a small clean brush, coat the entire surface with a thin layer of sauce (approximately ½ cup). Sweet sauces are loaded with sugars, so they'll give your Bacon Explosion a nice glossy finish. Spicy and vinegar-based sauces don't contain as much sugar, so they won't have that nice shiny look. To create the same effect, simply add 1 tablespoon honey to ½ cup sauce before glazing.

STEP 10: Using a sharp knife, cut the Bacon Explosion into ¼- to ½-inch slices to serve. If your roll was good and tight, you should now see a nice bacon pinwheel pattern throughout the sausage.

TO SERVE: Obviously pork is best served by itself, but if you feel the need to make this meat monster into a sandwich, try placing a couple Bacon Explosion slices on a warm biscuit. You'll reach pork nirvana in no time flat!

TIPS: When picking out raw bacon for your Bacon Explosion, look for uniform rectangular-shaped strips of bacon. Evenly sized strips of bacon will help your bacon weave be tight and uniform. We're extremely picky when it comes to weavable bacon, so don't hesitate to dig deep into the cooler at the grocery store. Sometimes the best slabs are stashed deep in the back!

If bulk sausage in unavailable in your area, you can easily cut the casings off of sausage in casing instead.

Bacon goes well with every drink in the book, but for the true bacon fiend, have a few shots of Bakon vodka on hand. You can order this online or at some retail outlets around the country. It also might be a good idea to have some regular light beer handy because the salt content in the bacon might make you a little thirsty!

BACON EXPLOSION BREAKFAST CASSEROLE

INGREDIENTS

10 slices white sandwich bread

8 eggs, beaten

4 cups milk

1 teaspoon dried mustard

2 cups grated sharp Cheddar cheese

2 cups chopped Bacon Explosion (page 43)

EQUIPMENT

13 x 9-inch casserole dish

Large mixing bowl

Wire whisk

Yield 12 servings

Now this never really happens at either of our houses so it's tough for us to relate, but on the rare occasion that you have some leftover Bacon Explosion, this is the perfect way to kick off the next morning with a second dose of pork.

STEP 1: Remove the crusts from the bread slices and discard. Cut each slice into four equal-sized squares.

STEP 2: Grease the casserole dish and line the bottom with the bread squares. It's okay if the squares overlap, just try to make a nice even layer of bread.

STEP 3: Combine the eggs, milk, and dried mustard in a mixing bowl.

STEP 4: Pour the egg mixture over the bread.

STEP 5: Evenly spread the cheese and chopped Bacon Explosion over the top of the entire casserole.

STEP 6: Bake uncovered at 350 degrees for 45 to 60 minutes.

STEP 7: The casserole is done when the top is evenly browned and the eggs are firm.

Try substituting 2 cups of your favorite cooked breakfast meat, chopped or crumbled, for the Bacon Explosion. Our favorites are bacon, ham, sausage, and Little Smokies.

What goes with breakfast better than a bloody Mary? A bacon bloody Mary of course! Remove the ridiculous celery from a regular bloody Mary and add a slice of super crispy bacon and a dill pickle spear. You're now in bacon breakfast heaven.

DOUBLE-DECKER BELT SANDWICH

INGREDIENTS

2 teaspoons mayonnaise

½ teaspoon barbecue
  sauce

3 slices white or wheat
  bread, toasted

4 leaves green leaf
  lettuce, washed and
  dried

4 ¼-inch slices tomato

4 ¼-inch slices Bacon
  Explosion (page 43)

EQUIPMENT

Toaster

Spoon

Sharp knife

Yield 1 sandwich

Every once in a great while you run across a recipe so grand that it actually taps all six sections of the food pyramid, and the Bacon Explosion Lettuce Tomato Sandwich just so happens to be one of them—assuming you drink a glass of milk with it, or better yet, add a slice of cheese. Diagrams don't lie, so let's break down the nutritional value of this meal:

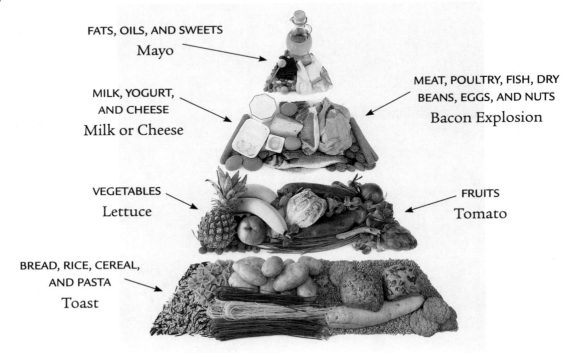

FATS, OILS, AND SWEETS
Mayo

MILK, YOGURT,
AND CHEESE
Milk or Cheese

MEAT, POULTRY, FISH, DRY
BEANS, EGGS, AND NUTS
Bacon Explosion

VEGETABLES
Lettuce

FRUITS
Tomato

BREAD, RICE, CEREAL,
AND PASTA
Toast

The next time your doctor tells you to watch your diet, just show him/her this simple diagram illustrating that you're acutely aware of your dietary needs and are proactively monitoring the situation. We're sure he or she will be extremely impressed by your efforts and will send you packing with a clean bill of health.

STEP 1: Combine the mayonnaise and barbecue sauce and spread half of the mixture on a slice of toast.

STEP 2: Top with 2 lettuce leaves, 2 slices of tomato, and 2 slices of Bacon Explosion.

STEP 3: Top with another slice of toast and repeat. Top with the last slice of toast.

TO SERVE: For a true deli feel, cut the sandwich on a diagonal and insert frilly toothpicks into each half. Serve with chips or Sweet-Potato Fire Fries (page 85), and a dill pickle spear.

Your favorite wheat beer will complement the bread and flavor of the sandwich as it goes down crisp and cold. For those of you that must have the original Kansas City feel, order up a pint of Boulevard Wheat with a lemon.

MOINK BALLS

INGREDIENTS

12 precooked Italian-
style meatballs

6 strips bacon, cut in half

1 tablespoon brown
sugar

⅛ teaspoon cayenne
pepper

½ cup barbecue sauce

½ cup grape jelly

EQUIPMENT

Smoker

Toothpicks

Tongs

Yield 6 servings (2 balls per person!)

I'm sure you're thinking "What the hell is a MOINK Ball?" Made popular by our friend Larry Gaian and his Web site thebbqgrail .com, MOINK Balls join together the two most popular proteins in the barbecue world—beef and pork. MOO+OINK=MOINK. These little delights have acquired quite the following in online barbecue forums, so it's only fitting that we give them the full-fledged shout-out in our bacon chapter. They're easy to make and are made even better with a simple jelly glaze. Plus it never hurts to serve a dish that makes people say, "Man, I love your balls!!!"

STEP 1: Wrap each meatball with a half strip of bacon and secure it with a toothpick.

STEP 2: Combine the brown sugar and cayenne pepper and sprinkle over the bacon-wrapped meatballs.

STEP 3: Smoke over indirect heat at 250 degrees for about 1 hour until the bacon is done to your liking.

STEP 4: While the MOINK Balls are cooking, combine the barbecue sauce and grape jelly in a saucepan and heat until blended.

STEP 5: Five minutes before removing the balls from the smoker, baste them with the glaze. Serve immediately.

This recipe also works great on the grill over direct heat for 10 to 15 minutes, although this method does require close attention. Bacon grease is highly flammable, so you will need to rotate the MOINK Balls constantly to prevent scorching.

Amber ale is your best choice here. With a medium flavor profile it won't overwhelm the tasty flavor of your MOINK Balls. Fat Tire Amber Ale is a regular in our arsenal.

According to Larry, "official" MOINK Balls must be made with precooked Italian-style meatballs that are found in the freezer section of your local grocery store. The beauty of this recipe lies in its simplicity, so don't let Larry catch you using homemade meatballs or he'll revoke your MOINK Baller Certification.

ATOMIC BUFFALO TURDS

INGREDIENTS

12 fresh large jalapeño
    peppers

8 ounces cream cheese,
    at room temperature

2 teaspoons paprika

1 teaspoon cayenne
    pepper

¼ cup crushed pineapple,
    drained

1 cup pulled pork
    (page 25)

12 strips bacon, cut in
    half

Sweet barbecue rub

EQUIPMENT

Smoker

Knife

Spoon

Mixing bowl

Toothpicks

Yield 12 servings

Those that frequent barbecue circles are all too familiar with the classic Atomic Buffalo Turd recipe (or as they're called online, ABTs). Adapted from the barfly favorite jalapeño popper (fried cream cheese-stuffed jalapeño peppers), the barbecue version replaces that crispy outer crust with a hefty dose of pork and a layer of smoky flavor, though there's one portion of the adaptation that we're not too fond of. When you bite down into an ABT, you might be surprised to find a little smokie hiding inside that pocket of molten cream cheese. For some, that mini hot dog might be exactly what the doctor ordered, but for us it leaves a lot to be desired. Don't get us wrong, hot dogs have their time and place (like at a baseball game), but the center of these smoked jalapeños should be reserved for bona fide barbecue meat. That's why we've swapped out those cocktail wieners in favor of juicy pulled pork.

STEP 1: Remove the stems from the jalapeños and slice each one in half lengthwise.

STEP 2: Using a spoon, remove the ribs and seeds.

STEP 3: In a mixing bowl, combine the softened cream cheese, paprika, cayenne pepper, and pineapple.

STEP 4: Gently stir the pulled pork into the mixture.

STEP 5: Using a knife or spoon, fill the jalapeño halves with the cream cheese mixture. If you're doing a large number of ABTs, try placing all of the cream cheese mixture into a large ziplock bag with one-half inch cut off the corner. You can then squeeze the mixture through the bag to fill the jalapeños much quicker.

STEP 6: Wrap each stuffed jalapeño with a half strip of bacon and secure each one with a toothpick.

STEP 7: Sprinkle with your favorite sweet barbecue rub.

STEP 8: Smoke at 250 degrees over indirect heat for about 1½ hours until the bacon is done to your liking.

For your beer choice, stick with Corona or Dos Equis. A light lager is a good counter to the jalapeños.

BACON GORGONZOLA TWICE-GRILLED POTATOES

INGREDIENTS

8 baby (2-inch) white Idaho potatoes

Olive oil

Salt to taste

8 strips bacon

1 cup sour cream

½ cup milk

4 tablespoons butter, at room temperature

½ teaspoon salt

½ teaspoon ground black pepper

½ cup Gorgonzola cheese crumbles

EQUIPMENT

Grill

Fork

Basting brush

Aluminum foil

Skillet

Sharp knife

Spoon

Handheld mixer

Yield 8 servings

It's no secret that baked potatoes are twice as good cooked on the grill than cooked in an oven. So if you were to grill them twice, does that make them four times better than their indoor counterpart? If so, then does adding bacon and Gorgonzola cheese push that number to eight times better than the standard baked potato? One bite of these morsels and your answer will be "YES!!!" To make these as a side dish to accompany a grilled steak (page 91) or chicken fillet (page 195), substitute the baby-sized potatoes for large baking potatoes.

STEP 1: Wash each potato and pierce the skin several times with a fork.

STEP 2: Lightly brush the potatoes with olive oil and sprinkle with salt.

STEP 3: Double wrap each potato in aluminum foil and grill over medium-high direct heat for about 30 minutes until tender, turning often.

STEP 4: While the potatoes are cooking, head back inside and fry the bacon in a skillet on the stove until crispy. Let cool and crumble.

STEP 5: Remove the potatoes from the grill, unwrap, and cut in half lengthwise.

STEP 6: Using a spoon, gently scoop the flesh of the potatoes into a bowl. Try to leave about an $\frac{1}{8}$-inch potato shell.

STEP 7: Using a mixer, blend the sour cream, milk, butter, salt, and pepper into the potatoes until creamy.

STEP 8: Gently stir in the Gorgonzola cheese.

STEP 9: Fill the potato shells with the mixture. Place skin side down directly on the grill and cook for 10 to 15 minutes.

STEP 10: Top with crumbled bacon before serving.

A nice Vienna lager is the way to go here. Sam Adams is a well known and widely available brew, while a Great Lakes Eliot Ness is our choice of the day.

SMOKY BACON CORN BREAD

INGREDIENTS

6 strips bacon

1 box yellow cake mix

1 box yellow corn bread mix

2 large eggs

⅓ cup milk

⅓ cup water

⅓ cup vegetable oil

EQUIPMENT

Smoker

Skillet

Paper towels

Small bowl

Large mixing bowl

8-inch square baking pan

Yield 9 servings

Corn bread is a lot like barbecue when it comes to regional styles and differences. In the northern parts of this country, corn bread trends toward a sweeter cakey version, while the southern regions lean toward a saltier fried version. While you'll never get these two parties to agree on which flavor is better, we've got one statement they're sure to embrace equally—bacon and barbecue both make corn bread better!

STEP 1: In a hot skillet, fry the bacon until crispy, then cool on paper towels. Pour the bacon drippings into a small bowl and reserve.

STEP 2: In a large bowl, mix together the remaining ingredients and let stand for 5 minutes.

STEP 3: Using a paper towel, liberally grease an 8-inch square baking pan with the reserved bacon drippings and pour the batter into the pan.

STEP 4: Crumble the fried bacon and evenly sprinkle it across the top of the batter. Gently press the bacon pieces so that they sink down into the batter.

STEP 5: Smoke over indirect heat at 350 degrees for about 30 minutes until a toothpick inserted into the center comes out clean.

This recipe also works great in a 350-degree oven for thirty minutes.

CANDIED BACON STRIPS

INGREDIENTS

12 strips bacon, cut in half

¼ cup pure maple syrup

¼ cup dark brown sugar

Cayenne pepper to taste

EQUIPMENT

Smoker

Basting brush

Bacon is meat candy, so it's only fitting to sugarcoat it and turn it into real candy. Whether you're serving these as an appetizer or dessert, it's a surefire way to win over a roomful of carnivores.

STEP 1: Brush both sides of the bacon with maple syrup and coat with brown sugar and cayenne pepper.

STEP 2: Smoke over indirect heat at 300 degrees for about 45 minutes until the bacon is crispy.

While we prefer to enjoy this recipe plain, you can also wrap these delicious strips of meat candy around chunks of pineapple before smoking to get your daily dose of fruit. Secure the bacon in place with a toothpick just as you would with MOINK Balls (page 54).

This recipe also works great in the oven. Simply place the bacon on a raised rack over a baking pan to catch the excess juices.

OLIVES STUFFED WITH BACON AND BLUE CHEESE

Yield 4 servings

INGREDIENTS

12 jumbo Spanish olives, pitted but not stuffed

Blue cheese crumbles

3 strips bacon, fried crisp and crumbled

EQUIPMENT

Smoker

Barbecue techniques don't make it into the drink world all that often, but when used correctly, the smoking process is a fantastic flavor enhancer that can be customized to complement just about any flavor imaginable. Toss a few of these olives into a bloody Mary or dirty martini, and you'll be ready for "Q" brand booze. But don't let our cocktail-centered minds fool you, these olives are great all by themselves.

STEP 1: Holding an olive in one hand, completely fill the interior by pressing blue cheese crumbles into the empty cavity.

STEP 2: Insert as many bacon pieces into the blue cheese as possible. You can also mix the bacon and blue cheese together before stuffing, but keep some bacon pieces sticking out the end so that everyone knows there's bacon inside these guys.

STEP 3: Place in a 225-degree smoker over indirect heat for 10 to 15 minutes.

BACON-WRAPPED ASPARAGUS BUNDLES

INGREDIENTS

1 pound fresh asparagus
   spears
¼ cup olive oil
½ teaspoon garlic powder
¼ teaspoon salt
¼ teaspoon ground black
   pepper
4 strips bacon

EQUIPMENT

Grill
Platter or cookie sheet
Toothpicks
Tongs

Yield 4 servings

Vegetables are good, but meat is better. Wrap your vegetables in meat, and now you've got a reason to keep up on the three to five daily servings that the USDA recommends.

STEP 1: Rinse the asparagus spears and remove the woody base by holding the spear by the cut end and gently bending. The spear will snap at the natural weak spot, leaving the tender edible portion.

STEP 2: Place the asparagus on a platter or cookie sheet, drizzle with olive oil, and turn to coat the spears evenly.

STEP 3: Combine the garlic powder, salt, and pepper and sprinkle over the asparagus.

STEP 4: Lay the bacon strips flat on a baking sheet.

STEP 5: Place one-quarter of the asparagus spears in the middle of each strip of bacon.

STEP 6: Tightly wrap the bacon around the center of the asparagus bundle and secure it in place with a toothpick. Repeat with the remaining asparagus and bacon.

STEP 7: Grill over direct medium-high heat for about 10 minutes, turning frequently until the bacon is crisp.

BACON BROCCOLI SLAW

INGREDIENTS

½ cup sugar

½ cup mayonnaise

¼ cup vinegar-based
   barbecue sauce

¼ cup olive oil

1 package chicken-
   flavored ramen
   noodles

1 bunch broccoli, washed
   and chopped

¼ cup chopped green
   onions

¼ cup shredded carrots

1 rib celery, finely diced

½ medium red onion,
   finely diced

6 strips bacon, cooked
   and crumbled

EQUIPMENT

Medium bowl

Whisk

Large bowl

Rolling pin

Gallon-sized ziplock bag

Yield 8 servings

The perfect side dish for summer picnics and hot summer nights. It's quick and easy to put together, and for the health conscious it has practically zero fat and cholesterol and is packed with vitamins. Of course, we have added bacon and barbecue sauce to make it even better! Chill this crunchy treat in a 1-gallon ziplock bag for easy transportation to your picnic.

STEP 1: In a medium bowl, combine the sugar, mayonnaise, barbecue sauce, olive oil, and seasoning from the package of ramen noodles. Whisk until smooth.

STEP 2: Crush the ramen noodles with a rolling pin. Combine the broccoli (both florets and stalks), green onions, carrots, celery, red onion, bacon, and crushed ramen noodles in a large bowl. Add the dressing and toss until evenly coated. Chill in a covered bowl or ziplock bag for at least 2 hours.

Some additional ingredients can be added based on your preferences. Unsalted peanuts, almond slivers, sunflower seeds, chopped water chestnuts, diced cranberries, and ground pepper are all good options.

BACON MAC AND CHEESE WITH FRENCH-FRIED-ONION CRUST

Yield 12 servings

This recipe came from an inspiration of our pig-loving friend Pamela Lund. And when we say pig loving, we're not joking. She has a collection of over 300 stuffed, ceramic, metal, and cardboard pigs. We suppose you could call her the "crazy pig lady" (sorry, Pam).

When she told us about this recipe, we originally thought of it as a side dish, but after making it (and adding a bit more bacon), we found it's a meal all by itself. No matter what the occasion, this casserole is top-notch bacon-cheesy goodness.

STEP 1: First we need to create the sauce, which is called béchamel (a base sauce in French cuisine). Melt 3 tablespoons of the butter in a medium saucepan. Stir in the flour. Stirring continuously, cook over low heat for 3 minutes. Gradually stir in the heated milk (the microwave works fine) and cook, stirring, over medium heat for 4 minutes. Reduce the heat and simmer for 3 minutes. It's important to stir continuously to prevent scorching.

STEP 2: Remove the sauce from the heat and add ½ teaspoon of the salt, the black pepper, Parmesan, and Tabasco. Mix until the cheese has melted. Cover and set aside.

INGREDIENTS

5 tablespoons unsalted butter

3 tablespoons flour

1½ cups milk, heated

1½ teaspoons salt

½ teaspoon ground black pepper

5 ounces Parmesan cheese, grated

½ teaspoon Tabasco sauce

12 strips bacon

1 pound elbow macaroni

2 cloves garlic, minced

16 ounces sharp Cheddar cheese, shredded

16 ounces Velveeta, cubed

1 can (6 ounces) French's Cheddar French Fried Onions, crushed

EQUIPMENT

Medium saucepan

Spoon

Skillet

Large pot

Colander

3-quart glass baking dish

Cooking spray

STEP 3: Cook the bacon in a skillet until just crispy and set aside to cool.

STEP 4: To cook the macaroni, boil a large pot of water and add the remaining 1 teaspoon salt and the noodles. Cook for 5 minutes until the pasta is firm but not hard (overcooking will result in mushy pasta after you bake it). Drain the noodles and return to the pot. Immediately add the remaining 2 tablespoons butter, the garlic, and your béchamel sauce. Toss well.

STEP 5: Preheat the oven to 375 degrees and spray a 3-quart glass baking dish with cooking spray. Place one-third of the cooked macaroni in the baking dish. Evenly top with one-third of the Cheddar, one-third of the Velveeta, and 4 strips of bacon broken into small pieces. Repeat until all noodles, bacon, and cheese are used.

STEP 6: Top the entire dish with crushed fried onions.

STEP 7: Bake for 35 to 45 minutes until the top is beginning to brown. Let sit for 5 minutes before serving.

The Cheddar French Fried Onions aren't always available. Substitute regular French Fried Onions, as those are easy to find.

BACON-WRAPPED PORK MEDALLIONS

Yield 6 servings

INGREDIENTS

2 pork tenderloins
    (1 pound each)
6 strips bacon
Plowboys Yardbird Rub

EQUIPMENT

Grill
Sharp knife
Toothpicks
Tongs

Plowboys Yardbird Rub has long been a staple in our spice rack, but we didn't get hooked up with its creator, Todd Johns, until he saw us using it on a local news channel's coverage of the Bacon Explosion. We're big supporters of local KC businesses and even bigger supporters of top-notch barbecue. The Yardbird Rub is a spicy balance of salt and sugar with plenty of paprika to give your barbecue a rich red color once cooked. We've shipped his rubs all over the world, so now Todd's sharing one of his championship pork recipes! This recipe earned the Pork Pullin' Plowboys the title of 2008 Missouri Pork Loin Champion as well as a top 10 finish at the 2008 Jack Daniel's Invitational in the "Anything But" category.

STEP 1: Slice each whole tenderloin crosswise into 3 equal-sized portions.

STEP 2: Take one portion and lay the cut edge flat on the cutting board. Holding a knife parallel to the cutting board, begin cutting the pork through the middle of the fillet. Stop cutting ½ inch before slicing all the way through and fold open the fillet. Repeat for the remaining portions. This style of carving is called butterflying, and it will double the surface area of your fillets while keeping a thickness ideal for grilling.

STEP 3: Wrap a strip of bacon around the outside edge of each fillet and secure the overlapping ends with toothpicks.

STEP 4: Season both sides of the medallions with a light dusting of Plowboys Yardbird Rub.

STEP 5: Grill over medium direct heat for 7 to 8 minutes on each side until the internal temperature of the pork reaches 145 degrees. Remove the toothpicks before serving.

To add a little extra flavor to this recipe, try using a premarinated pork tenderloin available at your local market.

Try a British-style bitter ale with your pork medallions. Honker's Ale from Goose Island or Foster's Special Bitter are easily found across the country.

CHAPTER 3

PARTIES AND TAILGATES

Behold, the tailgate party. The pinnacle of human achievement. Since the dawn of parking lots, man has sought to fill his gut with food and alcohol in anticipation of watching others exercise.

—Homer Simpson, *The Simpsons*

Coming from a town that boasts the title of "The Best Smelling Parking Lot in the NFL," it's no surprise that we're seasoned veterans when it comes to tailgating. Even when the Chiefs are nowhere near contending for a title, you can still bet that the parking lots of Arrowhead Stadium will be packed full of grills come Sunday morning.

Those who have experienced an Arrowhead tailgate know there's only one way to arrive on site. Whether it's a 100-degree August preseason outing or a -10 degree mid-January playoff battle, the windows get rolled down as soon as you hit the gates to let the sweet aroma of KC barbecue fill your car. As the attendants wind you through the maze of parked cars, the faint smell of barbecue smoke is slowly replaced with the distinct scent of searing meat.

When planning a parking lot party, there are a few simple things to keep in mind. Obviously picking out the food is top priority, but here are three quick tips for making your blacktop meat feast go off without a hitch.

1. **Beverages.** Who's kidding here?!?! The real reason we tailgate is to enjoy a few cocktails before heading in and paying the outrageous stadium/arena prices. It's just like "pre-drinking" in college. It's the drinks you have before you drink. Consider it alcohol appetizers.

2. **Preparation.** Generally speaking you'll want to have most, if not all, of your prep work done before arriving on site. This leaves more time for the aforementioned pre-drinking and also cuts down on the supplies you have to bring with you. The more items that you have to bring, the more likely you are to forget something critical. And since parking lots aren't the easiest places to round up supplies, it's safest to hedge this situation.

3. **Clean Up.** If your tailgate party runs a little long, which tends to happen after all that pre-drinking, the last thing you want to do is miss the start of the big game because you're packing up. To keep this from happening, you'll want to be able to break down your parking lot party as quickly as possible. This means using disposable EVERY-THING. If tables are needed, cover them with the cheapest plastic tablecloths you can find. Being able to pile everything on the table, wrap the plastic up around it, and throw everything away is well worth the 99 cents.

Now just because we've laid out the framework for a successful parking lot party doesn't mean that these recipes are reserved only for the blacktop. The recipes found in this chapter work great at any type of social gathering. They're tried-and-true staples among our families and friends, and will be for you too.

STEAK-WRAPPED SHRIMP

Yield 6 servings

Steak and shrimp is a classic combination perfectly suited for a fancy sit-down meal. But when it comes to party time, steak knives are one thing you might not want floating around a crowd. Thankfully, these delicious little surf and turf poppers give all the satisfaction of a hearty meal without the need for sharp utensils.

STEP 1: Prepare the sauce by mixing together the steak sauce, horseradish, and lemon juice in a mixing bowl. Set aside until you are ready to grill.

STEP 2: Using a sharp knife, slice the steaks into ¼-inch-thick rectangular strips that are 1½ to 2 inches long. Try to keep all of the strips as uniform as possible to promote even cooking.

STEP 3: To assemble, take a peeled shrimp and pinch the head and tail ends together. Tightly (but gently) wrap the steak around the shrimp perpendicular to the fold and insert a toothpick all the way through the shrimp to hold the steak in place.

STEP 4: In a small bowl, combine the salt, pepper, paprika, onion powder, garlic powder, chili powder, and red pepper flakes. Sprinkle the seasoning on the steak-wrapped shrimp.

INGREDIENTS

1 cup steak sauce

1 tablespoon prepared horseradish

1 tablespoon fresh lemon juice

2 pounds rib-eye steaks

2 pounds large shrimp, peeled and deveined

1 teaspoon kosher salt

1 teaspoon coarsely ground black pepper

½ teaspoon paprika

¼ teaspoon onion powder

¼ teaspoon garlic powder

¼ teaspoon chili powder

⅛ teaspoon red pepper flakes

EQUIPMENT

Grill

2 small mixing bowls

Sharp knife

Toothpicks

Tongs

STEP 5: Grill the steak-wrapped shrimp over direct medium-high heat for 2 to 3 minutes per side, searing all sides of the steak. If done properly, the shrimp will be firm, but not overdone, once the steak is browned.

STEP 6: Just before removing the shrimp from the grill, lightly glaze with the prepared sauce. Serve immediately with the remaining sauce on the side for dipping.

When picking out steak for this recipe, look for beef that has good marbling but not a lot of thick fat pockets. Slicing across these fatty areas will cause your strips to break apart.

A dark lager works well with any steak. Leinenkugel's Creamy Dark and Heineken Dark are good choices.

PTERODACTYL WINGS

Yield 2 large servings

There's no question that hot wings are one of the manliest foods the world has to offer. They're crispy, spicy, messy, and come with an unspoken man-law to never eat the vegetables that are served on the side. The only flaw in this meal is that you have to eat two dozen of those dainty chicken wings to satisfy a man-sized appetite. To address this problem, we've taken it upon ourselves to supersize this meatatarian classic. Rib lovers have long enjoyed their mammoth-sized dinosaur ribs, so it's only fitting that wing lovers join the prehistoric party with pterodactyl wings.

STEP 1: Break down the wings by cutting them apart at the joints and discarding the tips. This is done by inserting the edge of a knife into the joint and firmly pressing down. If done correctly, your knife will cut through the cartilage relatively easily. You'll know you've caught the edge of the bone if it becomes difficult to cut. Bending the joint and feeling where the ball and socket meet is a good way to determine the location of your cut.

STEP 2: Combine all of the marinade ingredients and pour it into a gallon-sized ziplock bag. Add the wings to the bag, seal, shake, and thoroughly coat with the marinade. Refrigerate for 6 to 12 hours. If you can, jostle the bag every couple of hours to make sure the wings stay coated in the marinade.

INGREDIENTS

2 whole turkey wings

MARINADE

1 cup zesty Italian dressing
¼ cup hot sauce
1 tablespoon paprika
1 teaspoon cayenne pepper
1 teaspoon ground black pepper

SAUCE

¼ cup hot sauce
3 tablespoons butter
1 teaspoon white vinegar
1 teaspoon paprika
½ teaspoon cayenne pepper
½ teaspoon garlic salt

EQUIPMENT

Grill
Knife
Gallon-sized ziplock bag
Tongs
Saucepan
Heavy-duty aluminum foil

STEP 3: Remove the wings from the bag and discard the remaining marinade.

STEP 4: Grill the wings over medium direct heat for about 15 minutes, turning occasionally.

STEP 5: In a saucepan, combine the sauce ingredients over medium heat and bring to a simmer. Do not boil.

STEP 6: Tightly wrap each wing portion in heavy-duty aluminum foil with one-quarter of the sauce mixture. Grill over direct low heat until the internal temperature reaches 170 degrees, or until the juices run clear, approximately 20 to 30 minutes.

STEP 7: Remove from the grill and open each foil packet, being careful of the hot steam. Let the wings sit for 5 to 10 minutes before coating with the remaining juices in the packet and serving.

For crispy skin, quickly sear the wings over high heat after removing from the foil packet. Reserve the juices and coat the wings once removed from the grill.

If chicken wings are more your style, you can substitute 2 to 3 pounds of chicken wings for the turkey wings. Chicken wings are smaller, so they'll only need to be grilled about 7 minutes before wrapping all of them together in one large foil packet.

The manliest food calls for the manliest beer. A German Maibock called Dead Guy Ale is an award-winning beer found in many commercial liquor stores. It will complement your dinosaur-sized wings.

KANSAS CITY CAVIAR

Yield 10 to 12 servings

It's nothing personal, but the barbecue capital of the world has instilled within us a deep love and pride for all things Kansas City. So you can see why eating something called Texas Caviar just doesn't settle well. Luckily, there's an easy solution to this problem—toss out the iconic Texas ingredient and replace it with something a little more Midwestern. A true authentic KC barbecue meal is not complete without a side of pit beans, so we'll be swapping out those traditional black-eyed peas in favor of a hearty dose of white beans.

STEP 1: Empty the canned corn and beans into a colander and rinse away the juices that were included in the can. Try to drain as much of the water as possible before transferring to a large mixing bowl.

STEP 2: Dice the tomatoes, onion, green peppers, and green onions and add to the bowl.

STEP 3: Finely mince the garlic cloves and add to the bowl. You can also use a garlic press if you have one available.

STEP 4: The jalapeños require a bit more care than the other veggies. We recommend wearing food-safe gloves during this step to prevent the juices from soaking into the pores of your skin, which can burn if you inadvertently rub your eyes or nose. If you don't have access to

INGREDIENTS

1 can (15 ounces) yellow corn
1 can (15 ounces) white corn
1 can (15 ounces) black beans
1 can (15 ounces) white beans
2 large tomatoes
½ medium white onion
2 medium green bell peppers
6 green onions, green tops only
4 cloves garlic
2 jalapeño peppers
½ bunch fresh cilantro, washed and dried
1 cup zesty Italian dressing

EQUIPMENT

Can opener
Colander
Large bowl
Sharp knife

food-safe gloves, just be sure to thoroughly scrub your hands with soap to wash away the capsicum oil. Cut the jalapeños in half lengthwise. Using a spoon, scrape out the seeds and ribs and discard. Finely mince the jalapeños and add to the bowl.

STEP 5: Finely mince the cilantro leaves and add to the bowl.

STEP 6: Pour the zesty Italian dressing over the vegetable mixture and stir until combined. For best results, refrigerate your Kansas City Caviar overnight before serving.

TO SERVE: Place in a large serving bowl alongside a heaping bag of tortilla chips.

To convert the recipe back to classic Texas Caviar, substitute a can of black-eyed peas for the can of white beans.

SMOKED DEVILED EGGS

Yield 24 deviled eggs

INGREDIENTS

12 large eggs

½ cup mayonnaise

2 tablespoons Dijon
    mustard

2 tablespoons drained
    prepared horseradish

2 tablespoons sweet
    pickle relish

Salt and pepper to taste

Paprika, for garnish

EQUIPMENT

Smoker

Knife

Mixing bowl

Fork

When thinking of barbecue, eggs generally aren't the first thing to come to mind. As it turns out, though, the outer shell lends itself perfectly to the smoking process. It's porous enough to let a mild smoky flavor pass through, yet plenty firm to maintain that familiar egg shape under heat. Once smoked, these little guys are a great snack on their own. Transform them into deviled eggs, and now you've got a side dish worthy of any occasion.

STEP 1: Smoke the eggs over indirect heat in a 225-degree smoker for 2 hours. The smoke needs to penetrate all the way through the shell in order for the interior to absorb the flavor, so don't hesitate to blast these guys with a thick cloud of smoke.

STEP 2: Remove the eggs from the cooker and refrigerate overnight. The eggs will actually be ready to use as soon as they're cool, but letting them sit overnight allows time for the smoke flavor to set in.

STEP 3: Peel the eggs and cut in half lengthwise, removing the yolks.

STEP 4: In a mixing bowl, mash the yolks and stir in the mayonnaise, mustard, horseradish, relish, salt, and pepper.

STEP 5: Using a fork, fill the egg white halves with the yolk mixture.

STEP 6: Garnish with paprika and refrigerate until ready to serve.

CRAB CAKE–STUFFED MUSHROOMS

INGREDIENTS

CRAB CAKES

1 egg, beaten

3 tablespoons butter, melted

2 tablespoons mayonnaise

1 tablespoon Dijon mustard

1 teaspoon Old Bay seasoning

1 teaspoon fresh lemon juice

½ cup seasoned dried bread crumbs

1 pound lump crab meat, any shell pieces removed

12 (2-inch) button mushrooms

¼ cup panko bread crumbs

DIPPING SAUCE

¼ cup mayonnaise

1 tablespoon mustard

1 teaspoon fresh lemon juice

½ teaspoon hot sauce

Yield 12 servings

Since the great state of Missouri is completely landlocked, tracking down shoreline quality seafood can be quite a challenge. Because we like a challenge, we've developed quite the affinity for fine seafood. Among our favorites is the famous Maryland crab cake. When we turned to the grill to create our own smoky version, our attempts resulted in way too many crab nuggets falling through the grates. To keep this expensive mistake from happening again, we stuffed the crab cakes inside of mushrooms to create these delicious little snacks.

STEP 1: In a mixing bowl, combine the egg, butter, mayonnaise, mustard, Old Bay, and lemon juice. Add the dry bread crumbs and gently mix until moist.

STEP 2: Gently fold in the crab meat, being extremely careful not to break up the lumps.

STEP 3: Cover the mixing bowl with plastic wrap and refrigerate for at least 1 hour.

STEP 4: Remove the stem from each mushroom and generously fill the caps with the crab cake mixture. Gently press the mixture into each mushroom before dipping the exposed crab cake in panko bread crumbs to form a crust.

STEP 5: On a well-oiled grill over medium direct heat, sear the crab cake side of the mushroom for about 5 minutes.

STEP 6: Flip the mushrooms and transfer to indirect heat. Close the lid and grill for 10 to 15 minutes longer until the mushrooms are tender.

STEP 7: To prepare the dipping sauce, mix together the mayonnaise, mustard, lemon juice, and hot sauce. Serve immediately.

EQUIPMENT

Grill
Mixing bowl
Spatula
Tongs

To add a smoky flavor, add wood to your heat source once the mushrooms are moved to indirect heat.

This recipe can be prepared indoors. Sear both sides of the stuffed mushrooms in a little olive oil in a skillet over medium heat, then bake in a 350-degree oven.

ROASTED RED PEPPER AND MANGO SALSA

INGREDIENTS

3 mangoes

1 large red bell pepper

1 medium jalapeño pepper

½ lemon, juiced

½ lime, juiced

1 tablespoon honey

Salt and pepper to taste

2 tablespoons chopped fresh cilantro

EQUIPMENT

Grill

Sharp knife

Tongs

Mixing bowl

Small bowl

Yield 2 to 4 servings

Inspired by Jason's wife's love of roasted red peppers, this salsa recipe is a perfect blend of sweet and heat. The mangoes and honey partner with the red and jalapeño peppers to create a great salsa to serve while you're waiting on the main course to make its way off the grill.

STEP 1: Mangoes contain a rather large and awkwardly shaped pit from which you need to carefully carve away the fruit before you get grilling. To do this, stand the mango on end with the narrow side pointed toward you. Starting from the top, gently run your knife through the fruit, letting your knife follow the edge of the pit. Repeat for the other side.

STEP 2: Slice the mango pieces into ½-inch-wide strips, leaving the skin in place for stability during the cooking process.

STEP 3: Now that the mangoes are ready, it's time we turn our attention to the grill. The first thing we're going to do is roast our peppers to bring out some of the natural sweetness that's hiding inside. Grill the peppers over medium-high direct heat, turning often, until the skins are blackened and blistered.

STEP 4: Remove the peppers from the grill, immediately place in a paper bag, and cool. Sealing the peppers inside the bag will trap the steam and help the charred skin peel away easier.

STEP 5: While the peppers are cooling, grill the mangoes over medium direct heat for about 2 minutes on each side.

STEP 6: Once the peppers have cooled, remove the charred skin by gently pulling it away from the flesh.

STEP 7: Using a knife, remove the stems and seeds from the peppers and discard. Dice the red pepper into ¼-inch cubes and the jalapeño into ⅛-inch cubes and place in a mixing bowl.

STEP 8: Peel away the skin from the mangoes and discard. Chop the remaining fruit into ½-inch cubes and add to the mixing bowl.

STEP 9: In another bowl, combine the lemon juice, lime juice, honey, salt, and pepper.

STEP 10: Add the juice mixture and chopped cilantro to the mango mixture and stir until well combined. Chill for at least 30 minutes before serving.

SMOKY JALAPEÑO CHEESE SQUARES

INGREDIENT

1 jar (16 ounces) sliced pickled jalapeño peppers
2 pounds grated Cheddar cheese
8 eggs

EQUIPMENT

Smoker
13 x 9-inch pan
Mixing bowl
Fork or whisk
Knife

Yield 12 servings

When it comes to a party snack, this is definitely our go-to recipe. These squares are easy to prepare, and people just demolish them instantly. The cooking process tempers the heat of the jalapeños, leaving the delicious pepper flavor to be absorbed by the cheese.

STEP 1: Drain the jar of jalapeño peppers and coarsely chop. Spread them on the bottom of a 13 x 9-inch pan.

STEP 2: Top the jalapeño peppers evenly with the grated cheese.

STEP 3: Crack all 8 eggs into a mixing bowl and beat until well combined. Pour the beaten eggs over the cheese in the pan.

STEP 4: Smoke over indirect heat at 350 degrees for 30 to 45 minutes until the cheese has melted all the way through.

STEP 5: Let cool until the cheese solidifies. Cut into squares before serving.

If your smoker or grill is filled to the brim cooking the main course, this recipe also works great in a 350-degree oven; bake for 30 to 45 minutes.

SWEET-POTATO FIRE FRIES

Yield 4 servings

INGREDIENTS

2 large sweet potatoes, cleaned

2 tablespoons olive oil

1 tablespoon brown sugar

½ teaspoon kosher salt

½ teaspoon ground black pepper

¼ teaspoon cayenne pepper

½ teaspoon pumpkin pie spice

EQUIPMENT

Grill

Knife

Mixing bowl

Small bowl

Tongs

No longer are sweet potatoes reserved only for Thanksgiving. This spicy grilled fry recipe is the perfect accompaniment to a juicy burger (pages 97 to 109).

STEP 1: Using a knife, slice the sweet potatoes into ¼- to ½-inch rounds and place in a mixing bowl.

STEP 2: Drizzle the olive oil over the potato slices and toss until evenly coated.

STEP 3: In a small bowl, combine the brown sugar, salt, black pepper, cayenne pepper, and pumpkin pie spice.

STEP 4: Sprinkle the spice mix over the potato slices and toss until evenly coated.

STEP 5: Grill over medium direct heat for about 5 minutes on each side until tender. Serve immediately.

To make your Fire Fries extra hot, add an additional ¼ teaspoon cayenne pepper to the spice mixture.

ONE MILLION BEAN SALAD

INGREDIENTS

⅓ cup apple cider vinegar

1 tablespoon honey

½ tablespoon Dijon mustard

¼ teaspoon ground black pepper

3 cans beans, any type you like

1 medium white onion, chopped

1 large clove garlic, minced

¼ cup olive oil

EQUIPMENT

Large bowl

Can opener

Colander

Yield 8 to 10 servings

Out of curiosity for why people limit their bean salad to a measly three types of beans, this recipe evolved into a bit of a personal challenge to include as many types of beans as humanly possible. Granted, the challenge typically results in eating leftover bean salad for every meal over the following week and a half, but it's a small price to pay for the personal satisfaction of combing the local grocery stores to unearth a new kind of bean. Here's what we've uncovered so far in our local markets:

green beans

wax beans

garbanzo beans

light red kidney beans

dark red kidney beans

white kidney beans

pinto beans

navy beans

white beans

black beans

black-eyed peas

great Northern beans

butter beans

lima beans

fava beans

Since not every occasion requires enough bean salad to feed an army, we've broken the recipe down to the proportions of a run-of-the-mill three-bean salad. But if you ever decide to test the bean limits of your local markets, just scale up the recipe by repeating the quantities for every three cans of beans you find.

STEP 1: In a large bowl, combine the vinegar, honey, mustard, and pepper.

STEP 2: Using a colander, rinse and drain the beans, making sure to remove as much water as possible.

STEP 3: Add the beans, onion, and garlic to the large bowl and top with the olive oil.

STEP 4: Stir gently until the ingredients are well coated. Refrigerate for at least 4 hours, stirring occasionally.

To add a little extra crunch to your salad, try adding ¼ cup chopped green bell pepper for every 3 cans of beans.

For a spicy bean salad, try adding ¼ teaspoon cayenne pepper or a minced jalapeño pepper.

GRILLED ASIAGO CHEESE CHIPS

INGREDIENTS

Grated Asiago cheese

EQUIPMENT

Grill
Aluminum foil
Cooking spray

Why eat cheese-flavored potato chips when you can have 100% pure cheese chips? These guys will add an enormous amount of flavor to your salsas and dips. And if you make some big enough, you can even use them in place of bread for your Bacon Explosion sandwich!

STEP 1: Lay a piece of aluminum foil on the grates of a grill over direct medium-high heat.

STEP 2: Lightly coat the foil with cooking spray and place a heaping spoonful of cheese on the foil. Leaving a few inches between the cheese piles, continue until the foil on the grill has as many cheese chips as it can hold.

STEP 3: Close the lid on the grill and cook for approximately 5 minutes until the cheese has melted and is beginning to brown. Remove the foil sheet from the grill and let cool.

STEP 4: Remove the chips from the aluminum foil and serve.

To add a smoky flavor to your chips, toss a handful of your favorite wood chips onto the hot coals before closing the grill lid.

Try changing the variety of cheese to switch up the flavor. Because of their lack of moisture, hard cheeses such as Parmesan, Romano, and aged Gouda work best.

This recipe also works great by broiling the cheese on a foil-lined cookie sheet for 4 to 5 minutes until the cheese is bubbly and browned.

GRILLED POTATO SALAD

INGREDIENTS

1½ pounds Yukon gold
  potatoes

2 tablespoons olive oil

1 teaspoon garlic salt

¼ cup Baconnaise

¼ cup mustard-based
  barbecue sauce

1 teaspoon kosher salt

1 teaspoon ground black
  pepper

1 tablespoon dill pickle
  juice

2 ribs celery, diced

¼ cup chopped green
  onions

4 hard-boiled eggs, diced

¼ cup crumbled cooked
  bacon

EQUIPMENT

Grill

Gallon-sized ziplock bag

Cooking spray

Tongs

Medium bowl

Whisk

Spoon

Yield 8 servings

Bacon . . . man's best friend. Bacon in general should just be combined with everything anyway, so we're taking this grilled potato salad to new heights with Baconnaise and some cooked bacon.

STEP 1: Cut the potatoes into 1-inch-thick slices. Combine the sliced potatoes, olive oil, and garlic salt in a gallon-sized ziplock bag and toss gently.

STEP 2: Grill the potatoes over direct medium heat for 2 minutes on each side until tender. Remove and set aside.

STEP 3: In a medium bowl, combine the Baconnaise, barbecue sauce, salt, pepper, and pickle juice. Whisk until smooth.

STEP 4: Cut the cooked potatoes into small cubes. Add the potatoes, celery, green onions, eggs, and crumbled bacon to the bowl and toss gently to coat. Chill for at least 4 hours.

Baconnaise is a specialty bacon-flavored mayonnaise. It can be purchased online and at a select number of nationwide grocery stores. You can use regular mayonnaise, but add an additional ¼ cup cooked bacon to keep the bacon flavor intact.

HONEY-SEARED BLACK PEPPER FILET

Yield 2 servings

This recipe is one of our favorite ways to grill a steak. The bold flavors of the red wine soak deep into the meat, while its acidity is hard at work tenderizing the beef. The seared honey caramelizes and envelops the steak in a slightly sweet crust to create a juicy and delicious meal that can't be beat.

STEP 1: Combine 3 tablespoons of the honey, the wine, garlic, and pepper in a shallow dish. Coat the filets on all sides in the marinade and let sit at room temperature for 20 minutes.

STEP 2: Create a two-zone cooking surface by setting up your grill to have high heat on one side and medium-low heat on the other.

STEP 3: Pat the meat dry and sear over direct high heat for 2 minutes per side.

STEP 4: Move the steaks over to the medium-low side and cook for an additional 6 to 8 minutes, or until the steak is cooked to your liking.

STEP 5: During the last minute, glaze with the remaining 1 tablespoon honey and sear again on both sides.

INGREDIENTS

4 tablespoons honey
3 tablespoons red wine
2 tablespoons minced garlic
1 teaspoon ground black pepper
2 4- to 6-ounce filets mignon
Salt

EQUIPMENT

Grill
Shallow dish
Tongs
Spatula
Basting brush
Small dish

STEP 6: Remove the steaks from the grill and let rest for 5 minutes. Salt and pepper to taste.

If you prefer your steak a bit more done, cook longer over medium-low heat to an internal temperature of 135 degrees for medium and 145 degrees for medium-well. Decrease the final sear to 30 seconds per side.

Having a cold beer after slaving over a grilled steak is a no-brainer for us. A crisp Bass Pale Ale is always an excellent choice. For all of you wine drinkers, steer toward a dry red wine like Cabernet or Shiraz.

CHAPTER 4

BURGER HEAVEN

Hamburgers! The cornerstone of any nutritious breakfast.
—Samuel L. Jackson, *Pulp Fiction*

Burgers are a staple at restaurants and casual backyard barbecues across the country. There's nothing like the sizzling sounds of ground beef on the grill or the juicy flavors of a perfectly cooked patty. It could be an onion-laced slider from White Castle or one of the cryptic creations from In-N-Out Burger. Though after reading this chapter, your favorite burger will be the one you cook in your own backyard.

There are certain foods that all people should be able to cook and burgers are one of them. They're one of the most commonly grilled meats, as well as one of the most incorrectly cooked. However, a few of our simple rules will take your burgers to a whole new level.

1. Don't ever use premade frozen patties. They might be convenient, but they're typically made from low-grade meat that dries out or burns before the center is fully cooked. We prefer to use a heaping portion of 85/15 ground sirloin found at the fresh meat counter in the grocery store. The fat will keep your burger juicy and moist, yet there's enough lean to prevent extreme shrinkage.
2. Season your meat! There's a universe of different seasonings that can take your everyday burger to a new state of being. Yes, burgers have been scientifically proven to increase your at-oneness-with-the-world level!
3. When making burgers, always press the patties 1 inch wider than the diameter of your bun with the center being slightly thinner than the edges. As the meat cooks and the fat

renders, the patties will shrink and pull to the center of the burger. If you compensate for this during patty construction, you'll end up with perfectly uniform burgers instead of grilled meatballs.

4. Always keep the lid of your grill closed while your burgers are cooking. We like our patties thick and meaty, so keeping the lid closed will trap the heat and create an oven effect that will help cook the inside of the burger while the outside is searing on the grates.

5. We live by the theory that the less you play with your meat, the better. This means that once you place your burgers on the grill, the only time they should be touched is when you flip them over. We flip our burgers once and only once. The less you're poking and prodding at the meat, the better chance you have of keeping all those flavorful juices trapped inside.

6. Whatever you do, DO NOT smash the burgers with your spatula while cooking. This is THE cardinal sin of burger grilling and is one of the biggest reasons for having a dry burger. While this does make the fire sizzle and smoke, you're squeezing out all the juices that give the burger its delicious flavor.

7. If you're glazing your burgers, always apply the glaze at the very end of the cooking process. Most barbecue sauces are made with sugar, which burns easily over the high heat of a grill. Applying your burger lacquer during the last two minutes of cooking will provide enough time for the sauce to reduce without scorching.

8. Melting cheese over a burger is always a great idea. The technique is just the same as applying a glaze in that you want to carry out this action at the very end of the cooking process. During the last minute on the grill, top each patty with a slice of cheese and close the lid. The trapped heat will soften the cheese just as the burgers finish cooking.

9. Checking your burgers for doneness is one of the most critical steps of the cooking process. Ideally you should be using an instant-read thermometer to check the internal temperature of the patties. If you don't have access to this equipment, you'll have to rely on time or feel to determine when your burgers are done. Regardless of how you're testing for doneness, here are a few tips for burgers cooked over medium-high direct heat:

- Rare (pinkish red center): 3 to 4 minutes per side or an internal temperature of 145 degrees. The burger will feel mostly soft with a slight firmness.
- Medium (mostly brown with a slightly pink center): 5 to 6 minutes per side or an internal temperature of 160 degrees. The burger will feel firm yet spongy and have juices forming on the surface.
- Well Done (thoroughly browned with no traces of pink): 7 to 8 minutes per side or an internal temperature of 175 degrees. The burger will be firm and the juices will be clear.

10. Always toast your buns. This may be more of a personal preference, but the crunchy texture of a toasted bun paired with a soft and juicy burger is a match made in heaven.

Now that you're armed with the tools for success, get out there and have fun building those burger masterpieces—and even more fun eating them!

ALL-AMERICAN STUFFED BURGER

Yield 4 burgers

INGREDIENTS

2 pounds ground sirloin
2 packets Hidden Valley
   Ranch dressing mix
4 slices American cheese
½ cup barbecue sauce
4 hamburger buns

EQUIPMENT

Grill
Spatula
Mixing bowl

We've been making these burgers for years, but they didn't get their name until we saw Guy Fieri demonstrating his burger skills on the Food Network. For his "All-American Burger," the first ingredient he unveiled was—chorizo?!? Now we don't claim to be the brightest knife in the box, but putting chorizo in an "All-American Burger" seemed a bit baffling. If you've ever traveled abroad and asked for ranch dressing, then you know why these are the real All-American Burgers.

STEP 1: Place the ground beef in a large mixing bowl and, using your hands, thoroughly combine the ranch dressing mix with the meat.

STEP 2: Form the seasoned beef mixture into 8 even-sized patties that are about 4 inches wide. We'll use two ¼-pound patties for each burger, so it's best to make them thin.

STEP 3: Place a slice of cheese on 4 of the patties. If the corners of the cheese are close to the burger's edge, tear them off and place on the center of the cheese slice. There should be about a ½-inch "no-cheese zone" around the edge of the patty so that we can seal it all inside the burger.

STEP 4: Stack another patty on top of the cheese and completely seal the edges where the 2 patties come together. Be sure to seal the burger as tightly as possible, otherwise the cheese will ooze out during the cooking process.

STEP 5: Grill the burgers over direct medium-high heat until they are done to your liking (pages 94 to 95).

STEP 6: Baste the burgers with barbecue sauce for the last 2 minutes of grill time. Serve on toasted buns.

The All-American burger calls for an all-American beer. Head down and grab an Old Milwaukee and celebrate the birth of beer in the United States.

A heaping pile of fried bacon will only make this burger better!!!

CREAMY MUSHROOM STEAKBURGER

Yield 4 burgers

The classic mushroom Swiss burger has been around for eons. While we do enjoy the holey member of the cheese family, it's no match for a hefty dose of cream cheese.

STEP 1: Place the mushrooms in a saucepan with the beef consommé and bring to a boil. Reduce the heat, cover, and simmer for about 20 minutes until the mushrooms are tender.

STEP 2: Drain the mushrooms and reserve ¼ cup of the beef consommé. Return the consommé to the saucepan, add the cream cheese, and combine over low heat, stirring constantly. Once combined, stir in the mushrooms.

STEP 3: Using your hands, thoroughly combine the ground sirloin and steak seasoning in a mixing bowl. Form the seasoned beef mixture into 4 even-sized patties.

STEP 4: Grill over direct medium-high heat until the burger is cooked to your liking (pages 94 to 95).

INGREDIENTS

2 cups sliced mushrooms

2 cans (10.5 ounces each) beef consommé

1 package (8 ounces) cream cheese

2 pounds ground sirloin

1 tablespoon steak seasoning

4 onion buns

EQUIPMENT

Grill

Saucepan

Spatula

Mixing bowl

STEP 5: Place each cooked burger on an onion bun and top with a generous portion of the creamy mushroom mixture. Serve immediately.

NOTE: Beef broth can be used in place of beef consommé, but we prefer the appearance of the clear consommé as opposed to a cloudy broth.

Due to the predominance of mushrooms, an American blonde ale is called for here. Look for Redhook Blonde or a Skinny Dip from New Belgium Brewery.

BLUE CHEESE BUFFALO CHICKEN BURGER

Yield 4 burgers

As we stated with the Pterodactyl Wings recipe (page 75), hot wings rank among the manliest meals of all time. It's only fitting that we package it in convenient burger form.

STEP 1: Combine the ground chicken, bread crumbs, blue cheese, and ½ cup of the hot sauce in a mixing bowl and refrigerate for 1 hour. This will give the bread crumbs time to absorb the moisture from the meat and hot sauce and act as a binder to hold your burgers together.

STEP 2: Remove the meat mixture from the refrigerator and form into 4 equal-sized patties.

STEP 3: Mix the garlic powder and butter together and spread on the buns.

STEP 4: Grill the burgers over direct medium-high heat for approximately 7 to 8 minutes per side until the burgers are well done. During the last 2 minutes of grill time, baste the burgers with the remaining ¼ cup hot sauce.

INGREDIENTS

2 pounds ground chicken

1 cup dried bread crumbs

½ cup crumbled blue cheese

¾ cup hot sauce

¼ teaspoon garlic powder

2 tablespoons butter, at room temperature

Salt and pepper to taste

4 hamburger buns

Lettuce leaves

Tomato slices

EQUIPMENT

Grill

Mixing bowls

Spatula

Basting brush

STEP 5: After turning the burgers, toast the buttered buns facedown on the grill for 2 to 3 minutes.

STEP 6: Place the cooked burgers on toasted buns and top with lettuce and tomato before serving.

Anytime a bottle of hot sauce comes into play, you know it's going to be spicy. We have two schools of thought here: accentuate the spice or counteract the spice. To accentuate, go with an American IPA like Sierra Nevada Celebration IPA. To cut back on the heat, grab a strong porter or stout. Again Sierra Nevada makes a nice stout to help battle the fire.

SALTIMBOCCA-STUFFED BURGER

Yield 4 burgers

INGREDIENTS

2 pounds ground sirloin

1½ teaspoons ground
   dried sage

Salt and pepper

4 slices provolone cheese

8 slices prosciutto

4 hamburger buns

EQUIPMENT

Grill

Spatula

Mixing bowls

We were first introduced to saltimbocca at a dinner party thrown by our wives. (Yes, we're admitting we attend dinner parties, and sometimes we like it.) We were skeptical at first, but once we found out it was steak wrapped around prosciutto and cheese, we were instantly sold. Although the classic recipe is a pan-seared roulade finished off in the oven, our barbecue-addicted minds immediately saw the potential for a great burger.

STEP 1: Combine the beef, sage, salt, and pepper in a mixing bowl.

STEP 2: Form the seasoned beef mixture into 8 even-sized patties that are about 4 inches wide. We'll be using 2 of these patties for each burger, so it's best to make them thin.

STEP 3: Top 4 of the patties with a slice of provolone cheese and 2 slices of prosciutto, making sure to keep the stuffing at least ½ inch from the edge of the patty.

STEP 4: Add another patty on top of the stuffing and completely seal the edges where the 2 patties come together. Be sure to seal the burger as tightly as possible, otherwise the cheese will ooze out during the cooking process.

STEP 5: Grill the burgers over direct medium-high heat until the burgers are cooked to your liking (pages 94 to 95). Sandwich the burgers in hamburger buns and serve immediately.

Pick your favorite pale ale. It's a great all-around beer that will complement the many flavors in this burger. A mild Merlot will also do nicely for a dinner party.

TZATZIKI LAMB BURGER

Yield 4 burgers

INGREDIENTS

1½ pounds ground lamb

1 small white onion, minced

1 clove garlic, minced

2 tablespoons chopped fresh parsley leaves

½ teaspoon curry powder

Greek seasoning

Hamburger buns

1 cup tzatziki sauce

1 red onion, sliced

1 tomato, diced

EQUIPMENT

Grill

Large mixing bowl

Spatula

Lamb has a distinctly different flavor than ground beef, and your taste buds will celebrate when it's topped with tzatziki sauce! With significantly less fat than its beefy counterpart, this zesty Greek-style burger will deliver something different to your backyard barbecue.

STEP 1: Place the ground lamb in a large mixing bowl and, using your hands, thoroughly mix the white onion, garlic, parsley, and curry powder with the meat.

STEP 2: Form the seasoned lamb mixture into 4 even-sized patties and sprinkle with your favorite Greek seasoning.

STEP 3: Grill the burgers over medium-high direct heat until they are cooked to your liking (pages 94 to 95).

STEP 4: Sandwich the patties on buns with ¼ cup tzatziki sauce, sliced red onion, and diced tomato. Serve immediately.

For the total Greek experience, place the burger and toppings in a pita and garnish with a slice of lime!

Red wine is the standard pairing with lamb, but this is barbecue and this is a burger. You'll want a rich, dark, malty ale to pair with this creation. Black Duck Porter from Greenport Harbor Brewing Company is one we highly recommend.

PEPPER JACK CHILE BURGER

Yield 4 burgers

INGREDIENTS

1 tablespoon olive oil

1 small red onion, finely chopped

2 cloves garlic, minced

2 pounds ground sirloin

Salt and pepper

2 poblano peppers

4 slices pepper Jack cheese

4 hamburger buns

EQUIPMENT

Grill

Small skillet

Mixing bowl

Spatula

Tongs

Sharp knife

At first glance you might think this recipe is for the fan of spicy food, but the recipe is actually much milder than it appears. In fact, the pepper Jack cheese is the spiciest ingredient. Poblano peppers have a slight heat, but nothing compared to jalapeños or serranos. Poblanos are large, meaty peppers typically used for chiles rellenos, or stuffed chiles, which makes them perfect for roasting and topping a large burger. If you need more heat in your burger, substitute jalapeños or serranos for the poblanos.

STEP 1: Heat the olive oil in a small skillet over medium heat. Add the onion and garlic and sauté for about 5 minutes until the onion is translucent. Remove from the heat and cool.

STEP 2: Place the ground beef in a large mixing bowl and, using your hands, thoroughly mix the onion mixture, salt, and pepper with the meat.

STEP 3: Form the seasoned beef mixture into 4 even-sized patties.

STEP 4: Place the peppers on the grill over direct medium-high heat and grill, turning often, until the skin is blackened and blistered.

STEP 5: Immediately place the peppers in a paper bag, seal, and let cool. Steaming the peppers inside the bag will help the charred skin peel away easier.

STEP 6: Once the peppers have cooled, remove the charred skin by gently pulling it away from the flesh. Using a sharp knife, remove the stems and seeds from the peppers and discard. Cut the remaining flesh into ½-inch strips.

STEP 7: Grill the burgers over direct medium-high heat until the burgers are cooked to your liking (pages 94 to 95). Place a slice of cheese on each patty for the last minute of cooking.

STEP 8: Place the cooked burgers on hamburger buns and top each generously with roasted poblano peppers. Serve immediately.

This is another spicy concoction that calls for a light ale or blonde ale to balance everything out. Try Red Brick Blonde from the Atlanta Brewing Company or your favorite local brew.

GUACAMOLE TURKEY BURGER

Yield 4 burgers

Just because you're a beef eater doesn't necessarily mean your guests will be too. Serve these alongside our All-American Stuffed Burgers (page 97), and you'll be sure to please everyone—except the vegetarians.

STEP 1: To make the guacamole, slice the avocados in half and remove the pits. Using a spoon, scoop the flesh into a mixing bowl and combine with the sour cream, cilantro, and lime juice. Stir in the chopped tomato and onion and season with salt to taste.

STEP 2: Place the ground turkey in a large mixing bowl and, using your hands, thoroughly mix the bread crumbs, egg, Worcestershire sauce, garlic salt, and pepper with the meat.

STEP 3: Form the seasoned turkey mixture into 4 even-sized patties.

STEP 4: Grill over direct medium heat for approximately 7 to 8 minutes per side until the burgers are well done (page 95).

STEP 5: Place each cooked burger on a hamburger bun and top with a generous portion of guacamole. Serve immediately with tortilla chips for any remaining guacamole.

Guacamole and turkey calls for a Pecan Ale from Abita Brewing in Louisiana.

INGREDIENTS

4 ripe avocados
2 tablespoons sour cream
2 tablespoons finely chopped fresh cilantro
2 limes, juiced
1 medium tomato, coarsely chopped
1 small white onion, finely chopped
Salt to taste
2 pounds ground turkey
¼ cup seasoned dried bread crumbs
1 egg, beaten
1 teaspoon Worcestershire sauce
1 teaspoon garlic salt
¼ teaspoon ground black pepper
4 hamburger buns

EQUIPMENT

Grill
Sharp knife
Large spoon
2 mixing bowls
Spatula

CHAPTER 5

FATTIES FOR EVERY OCCASION

A highbrow is the kind of person who looks at a sausage and thinks of Picasso.

—Sir Alan Patrick Herbert

We first learned about fatties when Jason took a cooking class from local barbecue chef Richard McPeake. The class touched on a variety of barbecue styles and techniques, but the biggest thing we took away from that weekend was the concept of a fatty. As it turns out, this concept would be the inspiration for our Bacon Explosion (page 43).

A fatty in its most basic form is a smoked roll of sausage. Imagine unwrapping one of those raw sausage packages that you see at the grocery store and cooking it in a smoker. That's all it is! Of course, no one can be satisfied with sausage alone, so most people are now pressing the sausage flat and wrapping it around an assortment of cheeses, vegetables, and other meats.

The name "fatty" can be traced back to the online forums found on the Web site www.BBQ-Brethren.com. A member that goes by the avatar "Bigdog" long ago referred to the process as "smoking a fatty," and the name stuck. Despite the blatant marijuana reference, the community has rallied around the concept and now supports daily interactions of people posting pictures and reviews of their fatty recipes.

Cooking fatties is an extremely easy process and great for the beginning barbecuer. Since the meat is always ground, the fatty is much more resilient compared to other barbecue meats. This makes them great for practicing fire control. Just be sure to keep these few things in mind when first venturing into the world of fatties:

1. All of our fatty recipes call for bulk or uncased sausage. This is done for two reasons. The first is that it allows us to create large "logs" instead of the small links that most people throw on a grill. And, second, casing prevents the smoky barbecue flavor from fully penetrating the meat. If bulk sausage is unavailable in your area, you can purchase cased sausage and remove the casing by slicing down the side of the sausage with a sharp knife. After uncasing all of the links, mash them together in a mixing bowl until they are combined.

2. When creating a stuffed or rolled fatty, a gallon-sized ziplock bag is the perfect tool for creating a uniform patty. Place the ground meat in the bag and use a rolling pin to press the meat evenly to all of the edges. To remove, cut both side edges of the bag and fold back the top flap of plastic. The extra plastic gives you an easy way to keep your hands clean while rolling the sausage into the fatty shape.

3. When adding filling to a fatty, always leave a 1-inch border of sausage around the edge. Once you have rolled the fatty up, this edge will allow you to easily pinch the ends and seam to seal your flavor inside. This step is especially important when sealing cheese inside. As soon as the cheese starts to melt, it will ooze out any little hole it can find. It's always best to take extra time to make sure your fatties are completely sealed before placing them on the smoker.

4. No matter how hard you try, air pockets will always be formed while rolling the fatty. To make sure the cooked fatty holds together once sliced, you need to squeeze out these air pockets before sealing up the edges and seams. This can be done by firmly grabbing the fatty in the middle with both hands and pressing the air pockets to the ends. Continue this process until you no longer feel air pockets in the fatty.

5. If you are wrapping your fatty in a bacon weave (page 44), always make certain to cook the fatty with the seam of the bacon weave facing down. The weight of the fatty will keep the bacon weave pulled tight and prevent it from pulling back during the cooking process.

Not only are fatties one of our favorite items to smoke, they're also one of the most requested items from our friends and family.

As far as what beer to summon up when cooking fatties, we'll cover all of them right here. German-style beers are always in order. If the fatty has a spicy flavor, aim for a hoppy pilsner like a Warsteiner. For the sweeter, more savory fatty, look for a good Schwarzbier like an Einbecker, or for something more common, some Sam Adams Black Lager.

JANUARY 1, NEW YEAR'S DAY: HOPPIN' JOHN FATTY

Yield 6 to 8 servings

Eating black-eyed peas as your first meal in a New Year is said to bring good luck. We, of course, prefer to make that meal even better with barbecue.

STEP 1: Heat the olive oil in a skillet over medium heat. Add the onion, bell peppers, and garlic and sauté until tender. Remove from the heat and cool.

STEP 2: Empty the contents of the skillet into a mixing bowl and add the sausage, black-eyed peas, bread crumbs, chili powder, paprika, salt, and lemon pepper. Using your hands, mash all of the ingredients together until a uniform mixture is created.

STEP 3: Form the mixture into a 2-inch-diameter log. A sheet of aluminum foil or plastic wrap will help mold the mixture into shape. Just be sure to remove the foil or plastic wrap before placing it on the grill.

STEP 4: Smoke the fatty at 250 degrees over indirect heat until the internal temperature reaches 150 degrees, approximately 2 hours.

STEP 5: Slice into rounds and serve with long-grain white rice.

INGREDIENTS

2 tablespoons olive oil

1 small onion, coarsely chopped

½ green bell pepper, coarsely chopped with seeds removed

½ red bell pepper, coarsely chopped with seeds removed

1 clove garlic, finely chopped

1 pound hot sausage

1 can (14.5 ounces) black-eyed peas, drained and rinsed

¼ cup seasoned dried bread crumbs

1 teaspoon chili powder

¼ teaspoon paprika

½ teaspoon salt

¼ teaspoon lemon pepper

EQUIPMENT

Smoker

Knife

Skillet

Mixing bowl

Aluminum foil or plastic wrap

JANUARY 14, NATIONAL HOT PASTRAMI SANDWICH DAY: REUBEN/RACHEL FATTY

INGREDIENTS

2 pounds ground corned
beef

½ cup sauerkraut,
drained

½ cup shredded Swiss
cheese

¼ cup Thousand Island
dressing

1½ teaspoons coriander
seeds, coarsely
ground

1 teaspoon coarsely
ground black pepper

1 teaspoon brown sugar

½ teaspoon garlic powder

Sliced rye bread, toasted

EQUIPMENT

Smoker
Small mixing bowl

Yield 6 to 8 servings

Most people are familiar with the traditional corned beef and sauerkraut Reuben sandwich, but did you know that Reuben has a sister named Rachel? Substitute pastrami for the corned beef and coleslaw for the kraut, and you've got a smoked variation that's equally tasty. Unfortunately ground corned beef isn't something that's readily available, so you'll probably have to purchase a whole corned beef brisket and grind it yourself in a meat grinder or food processor. If you don't have either of these pieces of equipment, try asking the meat department at your local grocery store to grind it for you.

STEP 1: Press out the ground corned beef into a ½-inch-thick square.

STEP 2: Evenly top the corned beef with sauerkraut, cheese, and Thousand Island dressing.

STEP 3: Roll up the corned beef layer, completely sealing the contents inside.

STEP 4: In a small mixing bowl, combine the coriander, pepper, brown sugar, and garlic powder to create a rub. Evenly sprinkle the rub on the outside of the fatty.

STEP 5: Smoke the fatty at 250 degrees over indirect heat until the internal temperature reaches 165 degrees, approximately 2 hours.

STEP 6: Slice and serve on toasted rye bread.

FEBRUARY 14, VALENTINE'S DAY: ITALIAN FATTY

INGREDIENTS

2 tablespoons olive oil

½ white onion, diced

1 red bell pepper, diced

1 clove garlic, minced

2 pounds bulk Italian
    sausage

½ cup shredded
    mozzarella cheese

Marinara sauce

EQUIPMENT

Smoker

Knife

Skillet

Yield 6 to 8 servings

What could be more romantic than a fine Italian dinner on Valentine's Day? This year there's no need to pay big bucks at a crowded fancy restaurant when an even better dinner can be made in your backyard.

STEP 1: In a skillet, heat the olive oil over medium heat. Add the onion, pepper, and garlic and sauté until tender. Remove from the heat and let cool.

STEP 2: Press the sausage into a ½-inch-thick square.

STEP 3: Evenly top with the vegetable mixture and cheese.

STEP 4: Roll up the sausage layer, completely sealing the contents inside.

STEP 5: Smoke the fatty at 250 degrees over indirect heat until the internal temperature reaches 150 degrees, approximately 2 hours.

STEP 6: While the fatty is cooking, simmer any marinara sauce to be used when plating. Slice the fatty and serve over warm pasta with sauce and toasted garlic bread.

A fancy Italian dinner calls for a tall glass of wine. Reach for a Dolcetto for this special occasion.

EVERY DAY: CHEESY JALAPEÑO FATTY

INGREDIENTS

2 pounds bulk Italian sausage

½ cup pickled jalapeño peppers, sliced

1 cup shredded Provel cheese

EQUIPMENT

Smoker

Yield 6 to 8 servings

After making a basic fatty, this was the first stuffed version we created. The creamy Provel cheese is a perfect pairing with the juicy Italian sausage. The whole thing comes together with a touch of heat from the jalapeño peppers.

STEP 1: Press the sausage into a ½-inch-thick square.

STEP 2: Evenly top the meat with the jalapeños and cheese.

STEP 3: Roll up the sausage and completely seal the contents inside.

STEP 4: Smoke the fatty at 250 degrees over indirect heat until the internal temperature reaches 150 degrees, approximately 2 hours.

STEP 5: Slice and serve.

EASTER: SCOTCH EGG FATTY

Yield 6 to 8 servings

INGREDIENTS

2 pounds bulk sage
    sausage
5 hard-boiled (or
    smoked, page 79)
    eggs, peeled
½ cup panko bread
    crumbs
Sliced rye bread, toasted

EQUIPMENT

Smoker
Wax paper

Ever wonder what to do with all those leftover hard-boiled Easter eggs? How about wrapping them in sausage and slow smoking them to perfection? Sure beats a salad topper, eh?

STEP 1: Press the sausage into a ½-inch-thick square.

STEP 2: Place the eggs end-to-end to form a line across the sausage square. The line of eggs should be an inch or two away from the front edge of the sausage square.

STEP 3: Gently peel up the front edge of the sausage square and roll up and over the eggs. Continue rolling until the eggs are completely wrapped in a layer of sausage. Pinch together the edges and seam to seal the eggs inside.

STEP 4: Gently pick up the fatty and place on a piece of wax paper coated with bread crumbs. Roll the fatty back and forth over the crumbs to form a crust around the outside of the sausage.

STEP 5: Smoke the fatty at 250 degrees over indirect heat until the internal temperature reaches 150 degrees, approximately 2 hours.

STEP 6: Slice and serve on toasted rye bread.

FOURTH OF JULY: BACON CHEESEBURGER FATTY

INGREDIENTS

10 strips thick-cut bacon

1½ pounds ground sirloin

1½ teaspoons ketchup

1½ teaspoons yellow mustard

½ cup shredded American cheese

2 pickle spears

Hamburger buns

EQUIPMENT

Smoker

Yield 6 to 8 servings

July Fourth is the biggest grilling holiday of the year. This year try replacing those plain ole grilled burgers with our smoked Bacon Cheeseburger Fatty.

STEP 1: Just like the Bacon Explosion, you need to create a 5 x 5-inch bacon weave. Take a look at the Bacon Explosion recipe (page 44) for details on creating a bacon weave.

STEP 2: Press the ground beef into a ½-inch-thick layer on top of the bacon weave.

STEP 3: Evenly top with the ketchup, mustard, and cheese.

STEP 4: Place the pickle spears 1 inch inside the front edge of the ground beef and roll the beef layer forward, leaving the bacon weave in place. Once the beef layer is rolled up, pinch together the ends and seam to completely seal the contents inside.

STEP 5: Roll the sealed fatty toward you, wrapping it in the bacon weave.

STEP 6: Smoke the fatty at 250 degrees over indirect heat until the internal temperature reaches 165 degrees, approximately 2 hours.

STEP 7: Slice and serve on hamburger buns.

OKTOBERFEST: BRATWURST FATTY

INGREDIENTS

2 pounds bratwurst

1 cup sauerkraut, drained

2 tablespoons spicy
brown mustard

Yield 6 to 8 servings

EQUIPMENT

Smoker

It's hard to dislike a country that enjoys beer and sausage as much as the Germans do. Adding barbecue is the only way we can make this glorious festival any better!

STEP 1: Remove the casings from the bratwurst and combine. Press the meat into a ½-inch-thick square.

STEP 2: Evenly top the meat with the sauerkraut and mustard.

STEP 3: Roll up the meat and completely seal the contents inside.

STEP 4: Smoke the fatty at 250 degrees over indirect heat until the internal temperature reaches 150 degrees, approximately 2 hours.

STEP 5: Slice and serve with a lager.

To take this recipe to the extreme, wrap the cooked fatty in pretzel dough (page 127) and bake until crisp!

THANKSGIVING: TURKEY AND STUFFING FATTY

Yield 6 to 8 servings

If there's two things we like most about Thanksgiving it's turkey and stuffing. The next time the holiday rolls around, make this Thanksgiving fatty as an alternative to the traditional roasted bird.

STEP 1: We're big fans of Stove Top stuffing, so that's the brand we always reach for when preparing this recipe. To start things off, prepare 2 cups of stuffing according to the instructions on the box and set aside. If you prefer homemade, or even another brand of instant stuffing, feel free to substitute your favorite.

STEP 2: In a mixing bowl, combine the ground turkey, melted butter, garlic powder, onion powder, white pepper, and poultry seasoning.

STEP 3: Press the turkey mixture to create an 8-inch square.

STEP 4: Evenly top the meat with the stuffing.

STEP 5: Roll up the turkey layer and completely seal the stuffing inside.

STEP 6: Smoke the fatty at 250 degrees over indirect heat until the internal temperature reaches 165 degrees, approximately 2 hours.

INGREDIENTS

2 cups Stove Top stuffing

2 pounds ground turkey

4 tablespoons salted butter, melted

½ tablespoon garlic powder

½ tablespoon onion powder

½ tablespoon white pepper

½ tablespoon poultry seasoning

EQUIPMENT

Smoker

Mixing bowl

DECEMBER 25, CHRISTMAS DAY: BREAKFAST FATTY

INGREDIENTS

2 pounds maple sausage

2 eggs, scrambled

½ pound bacon, fried and drained

½ cup shredded Cheddar cheese

EQUIPMENT

Smoker

Skillet

Yield 6 to 8 servings

Christmas morning we get together with our families and enjoy a breakfast feast. Since not all members of our families are as open to eating ribs and brisket before noon as we are, we cook this breakfast fatty as a way of bringing barbecue to Christmas.

STEP 1: Press the sausage into a 10-inch square.

STEP 2: Evenly top the sausage with the scrambled eggs, breaking up any large pieces. Crumble the cooked bacon and evenly sprinkle it over the eggs. Top it off with an even layer of cheese.

STEP 3: Roll up the sausage and completely seal the contents inside.

STEP 4: Smoke the fatty at 250 degrees over indirect heat until the internal temperature reaches 150 degrees, approximately 2 hours.

PRETZEL-WRAPPED FATTY

Yield Enough dough for 2 fatty halves

Soft pretzels have long been one of our favorite snacks. Stuff them full of leftover fatties and now you've got the ultimate snack.

STEP 1: Combine the water, soda, sugar, and salt in a small bowl. Sprinkle the yeast on top of the mixture and let stand for 10 minutes.

STEP 2: Combine the flour and butter in a large bowl. Pile the flour mixture in the middle of the bowl and, using your finger, make a well in the center of the pile. Pour the yeast mixture into the well.

STEP 3: Use a spatula to mix and form the ingredients into a dough. Knead the dough until smooth, approximately 7 to 8 minutes, until it cleanly pulls away from the sides of the bowl.

STEP 4: Remove the dough from the bowl and lightly coat the bowl with cooking spray. Return the dough to the bowl, cover and let rest until it doubles in size, approximately 1 hour.

STEP 5: While the dough is rising, preheat the oven to 450 degrees and line a baking sheet with parchment paper. In a large stockpot or roasting pan, combine the water and baking soda and bring to a boil.

INGREDIENTS

1 cup warm water (115 degrees)

½ cup lemon-lime soda, at room temperature

1 tablespoon sugar

2 teaspoons kosher salt

1 tablespoon active dry yeast

5 cups all-purpose flour

4 tablespoons unsalted butter, melted

10 cups water, plus 1 tablespoon

⅔ cup baking soda

1 leftover fatty, cut in half

1 egg yolk

Kosher salt to taste

EQUIPMENT

Small bowl

Large bowl

Spatula

Cooking spray

Baking sheet

Parchment paper

Stockpot

Basting brush

STEP 6: Once risen, place the dough on a lightly oiled work surface and divide into 2 equal portions. Press each portion into a 12 x 6-inch rectangle and top with half a fatty. Pull the side edge up, completely sealing the fatty inside. Flip the dough-wrapped fatty over so that the seam now faces down. Repeat for the second half.

STEP 7: One at a time, lower the dough-wrapped fatty into the baking soda bath for 30 to 45 seconds. Remove from the hot water and place on the parchment paper–lined baking sheet.

STEP 8: In a small bowl, combine the egg yolk and 1 tablespoon water. Using a basting brush, lightly coat the outside of the dough and sprinkle with kosher salt to taste.

STEP 9: Place the baking sheet in the oven and bake until browned, approximately 15 minutes. Slice and serve.

For smaller portions, wrap sliced fatty rounds instead of the whole log.

CHAPTER 6

THE LIQUOR SHELF

Well you see, Norm, it's like this. . . . A herd of buffalo can only move as fast as the slowest buffalo and when the herd is hunted, it is the slowest and weakest ones at the back that are killed first. This natural selection is good for the herd as a whole, because the general speed and health of the whole group keeps improving by the regular killing of the weakest members. In much the same way, the human brain can only operate as fast as the slowest brain cells. Now, as we know, excessive drinking of alcohol kills brain cells. But naturally, it attacks the slowest and weakest brain cells first. In this way, regular consumption of beer eliminates the weaker brain cells, making the brain a faster and more efficient machine. And that, Norm, is why you always feel smarter after a few beers.

—Cliff Clavin, *Cheers*

Beef. It's what's for dinner. Beer. It's what's for dinner too. Not a barbecue goes by without us worrying if we have enough beer and liquor. Be it a backyard party or a major competition, it's an ever-present concern. You could even go as far as saying that liquor is required. Many competition teams, including ours, participate in the early-morning good-luck shot. At 10 AM-ish we'll break out the Crown Royal and raise a toast in hopes that the judges like our meat.

With this attitude in mind, think of all the great flavors liquor can bring to a grilled meal. Depending on how often you dip into your liquor shelf, there's a chance that you've got a few bottles of booze leftover from past gatherings. We suggest trying them out in a few of our liquor-based recipes. Who knows? Before too long you might even begin buying booze for the sole purpose of cooking!

CAPTAIN MORGAN PIRATE BONES

Yield 2 to 4 servings

Put a little "grog" into yer ribs with this pirate-inspired recipe. Remember all those tips we gave you back in chapter one? Well those same rules apply here, except we'll be infusing the ribs with the smooth flavor of Captain Morgan Spiced Rum. Don't hesitate to apply the rub to your ribs the night before you plan to cook them. This will give the seasonings plenty of time to penetrate deep into the meat.

STEP 1: Trim away any remaining loose fat from the ribs and slather the slab with the honey and mustard.

STEP 2: Thoroughly coat the ribs with the pork rub to create a paste with the honey-mustard. Massage the mixture into the meat.

STEP 3: Smoke, using a mixture of apple and cherry wood, over indirect heat at 225 degrees.

STEP 4: After 2 hours of cooking, double wrap the slab in heavy-duty aluminum foil and add 2 tablespoons rum. Completely seal the foil packet and return the ribs to the smoker.

INGREDIENTS

1 slab (4 to 6 pounds) baby back pork ribs

1 tablespoon honey

1 tablespoon yellow mustard

½ cup pork rub

2 tablespoons Captain Morgan Spiced Rum

½ cup sweet Kansas City–style barbecue sauce

EQUIPMENT

Smoker

Cherry wood

Apple wood

Heavy-duty aluminum foil

Basting brush

STEP 5: After 2 additional hours of cooking, open the foil packets and use the bend test (page 20) to check for doneness. If the slab is done to your liking, glaze with the barbecue sauce and return to the smoker for another 15 minutes to set the sauce. If the slab is not quite done, return to the smoker for another 30 minutes to continue cooking. Repeat this process until the ribs are done to your liking.

STEP 6: Remove the ribs from the smoker, slice, and serve.

Ribs are best served with a lager that strikes a good balance with the pork. Sam Adams Light Lager is a commonly available choice. For the beer connoisseur, try Johnny Rawton American Pale Lager from Dogfish Head Craft Brewery.

If you want to keep your pirate roots intact, go all out and serve with Captain Morgan and Coke!

ABSOLUT PEPPAR DINOSAUR RIBS

Yield 4 servings

INGREDIENTS

¾ cup V8 juice

¼ cup Absolut Peppar vodka

1 teaspoon prepared horseradish

1 teaspoon fresh lemon juice

1 teaspoon Worcestershire sauce

1 rack (3 to 4 pounds) beef back ribs

1 shaker favorite beef rub

1 tablespoon hot sauce (optional)

1 bottle favorite barbecue sauce

EQUIPMENT

Smoker

Hickory wood

Heavy-duty aluminum foil

Basting brush

Whether we're dealing with pirates or dinosaurs, the rules for cooking ribs don't change. We won't bother repeating ourselves, so return to page 20 if you need a quick refresher course.

Now that you're back up to speed, let's head into the prehistoric age and re-create how cavemen satisfied their huge hunger for barbecue. Dinosaur ribs are a much tougher cut of meat compared to their pork counterpart. This has a tendency to scare a few people off, but it really only means that you'll have to cook them a little longer to get the desired tenderness.

A sweet and spicy barbecue sauce and rub work the best with beef ribs. To create the perfect combination, use a sweet barbecue sauce and a rub with some serious kick!

STEP 1: Mix the V8, vodka, horseradish, lemon juice, and Worcestershire sauce together and pour over the rack of ribs. This can be done on a cookie sheet, in a foil packet, or on plastic wrap. Cover and refrigerate overnight.

STEP 2: The next day, take the rack of ribs out of the refrigerator and remove them from the marinade. Massage a thick coat of beef rub deep into the meat of the ribs. You have the option of bringing the meat to room temperature first. Putting the ribs on cold allows more of the smoke to penetrate while cooking. It's all about how much smoke flavor you like!

STEP 3: Place the ribs in a 225-degree smoker over indirect heat and toss a few chunks of hickory wood into the firebox. Dinosaur meat has a strong flavor, so the bold hickory smoke will complement it well.

STEP 4: After the ribs have smoked for 2 hours, wrap the ribs in heavy-duty aluminum foil and return them to your 225-degree smoker over indirect heat. The foil creates a steam packet around the ribs, creating a moist and tender final product. If you want to add some extra flavor, throw 1 tablespoon of your favorite hot sauce in with the ribs. The steam will pick up the flavor of the sauce and drive it deep into the meat.

STEP 5: After cooking the ribs for 3 hours in the foil, unwrap the slab of ribs and return it to the smoker. This is the point at which you need to start testing for doneness. Dinosaur ribs normally take about 6 hours to be properly cooked, but that varies with each slab. You're shooting for an internal temperature of close to 200 degrees. The true test for doneness is tenderness. If the meat easily pulls away from the bone, they're ready to be taken off the grill.

STEP 6: Lightly glaze the ribs with your favorite sauce (preferably a spicy tomato-based one) and serve.

JAMAICAN RUM-AND-COKE CHICKEN

Yield 4 servings

The island lifestyle is all about living slow and savoring the spicy flavor of jerk chicken, at least that's what the lady working the snack bar of our Sandals Jamaican resort told us. We, on the other hand, couldn't get over the unique flavor of the local rum. It's as distinctive as the locals selling "necklaces" made out of conch shells. Match that bold flavor of island rum with the iconic jerk chicken, and you can bring a piece of paradise into your suburban backyard or big city apartment.

STEP 1: Trim any excess fat from the chicken and lay each breast between 2 pieces of plastic wrap. Using the blunt side of a meat tenderizer, flatten the chicken breasts until they're a uniform thickness throughout. Aim for a thickness between ¼ and ½ inch. This helps the chicken cook evenly and keeps the ends from drying out before the center is cooked.

STEP 2: In a bowl, combine the rum and Coke. Place the chicken breasts in the mixture and marinate in the refrigerator for 2 to 4 hours.

STEP 3: Remove the chicken breasts from the marinade and coat liberally with Jamaican jerk seasoning.

INGREDIENTS

4 boneless, skinless chicken breast halves

¼ cup Appleton's Golden Jamaican Rum (or other dark rum)

1 can (12 ounces) Coca-Cola

Jamaican jerk seasoning to taste

EQUIPMENT

Grill

Meat tenderizer hammer

Bowl

Tongs

STEP 4: Grill over high heat until the internal temperature reaches 165 degrees or until the juices run clear.

When there is five feet of snow on the ground and conditions are not perfect for island dwellers, this recipe also works great on a countertop grill or in a 375-degree oven for 25 to 30 minutes on a raised rack.

If you've ever been to Jamaica, then you know there's only one drink that goes with jerk chicken: a luke-warm bottle of Red Stripe beer. Apparently refrigeration is a lost cause in that part of the world, so the locals make do with the hand they are dealt.

HOT DAMN BUTTERNUTS

Yield 2 to 4 servings

INGREDIENTS

1 butternut squash

¼ cup Hot Damn or
    any other brand of
    cinnamon schnapps

1 tablespoon brown
    sugar, plus more for
    sprinkling

Kosher salt

EQUIPMENT

Grill

Sharp knife

Spoon

Basting brush

Easy there hot pants, get your mind out of the gutter. This recipe is not what you think. We're simply kickin' it veggie style this time around. Squash is one of our favorites, and it only gets better when grilled and brushed with booze.

STEP 1: Using a sharp knife, cut the squash in half lengthwise. Using a large spoon, remove the seeds and strings from the cavity at the base. Leave the rind on as this will help protect the flesh from scorching over the heat of the grill.

STEP 2: Score the inside of each half by making shallow, short cuts into the flesh. This allows the cinnamon and sugar flavors to soak down into the squash.

STEP 3: With the cinnamon schnapps, brush the scored squash and fill the hollow cavity of the butternut halfway to the edge. Sprinkle each half with ½ tablespoon brown sugar and a dash of kosher salt.

STEP 4: Grill over direct medium heat for 45 to 60 minutes. Every 10 to 15 minutes, brush with additional schnapps. Once a fork can easily slide through the squash, remove them from the grill and sprinkle with another layer of brown sugar. Serve immediately.

This recipe can also be prepared in a 375-degree oven for the same amount of time, but you'll lose the great smoky flavor the barbecue grill adds.

We're going to make a suggestion that you might have a little trouble pronouncing, but it's a perfect complement to this dish. Gewürztraminer (Ge-VERTZ-tra-MEE-ner—we know, it's hard to say) is what you're looking for here.

APPLEJACK PORK LOIN

Yield 2 servings

This recipe needs no introduction. Pork + Whiskey = Heaven.

STEP 1: In a large plastic container or a baking pan, mix together the bourbon, cider, apple butter, garlic powder, and Worcestershire sauce. Add the pork and turn to coat. Cover and refrigerate overnight.

STEP 2: The next day, remove the pork from the marinade, pat dry, and season with salt and pepper.

STEP 3: Grill over direct medium heat for about 30 minutes until the internal temperature reaches 145 degrees and the pork is tender and no longer pink.

STEP 4: If you need something a bit more potent, try mixing 3 parts maple syrup with 1 part Jack Daniel's to create a glaze. This can be basted on the pork loin toward the end of the cooking process or just drizzled over the sliced portions right before serving.

INGREDIENTS

¼ cup Jack Daniel's bourbon whiskey

¼ cup apple cider

½ cup apple butter (found in the jelly section at the grocery store)

½ teaspoon garlic powder

½ teaspoon Worcestershire sauce

1 boneless pork tenderloin, approximately 1 pound

Salt and pepper

Maple syrup (optional)

EQUIPMENT

Grill

Large container

Tongs

If you want to take this recipe one step further, try smoking it over indirect heat at 225 degrees with apple wood. It takes about 30 to 45 minutes longer to cook, but man is it worth the wait!

Here's where we run into our first dilemma. Beer or wine? Well, if you're throwing it on a sandwich, then beer for sure, but if you're serving it with a little romance, stick with wine. A hearty beer would bring balance and harmony to this recipe. St. Peter's Cream Stout or a rich porter immediately come to mind. For your wine, any Chardonnay would be an excellent pick.

GRILLED CHOPPED CHICKEN WITH VODKA SAUCE

Yield 4 servings

This recipe is unique and more of a "fine dining" dish usually found in an Italian restaurant. The best part, however, is that it's still barbecue! One thing we should stress before we get started: prepare the sauce at a low temperature. Sauces that include heavy cream are easy to scorch.

STEP 1: Peel back the skin on the chicken thighs and rub them down with your favorite poultry rub. Fold the skin back over the meat. Keeping the skin on will keep the juices in. (Later we'll be removing the skin, so don't worry about seasoning the outside.) Set the seasoned thighs aside.

STEP 2: Melt the butter in a saucepan over medium heat. Add the onion and garlic and sauté until the onion is soft and slightly brown.

STEP 3: Add the vodka and simmer for 10 minutes.

STEP 4: Stir in the tomato sauce and ¼ cup parsley. Bring to a boil, then decrease the heat and simmer for 30 minutes.

STEP 5: Add the cream and simmer for an additional 30 minutes. Stir frequently or the cream will start to clump.

INGREDIENTS

12 chicken thighs
Poultry rub
½ cup unsalted butter
¼ cup chopped onion
1 tablespoon minced garlic
1 cup vodka
4 cups tomato sauce
¼ cup fresh parsley, chopped, plus more for garnish
2 cups heavy cream
Chopped fresh parsley
Grated Parmesan cheese

EQUIPMENT

Grill
Saucepan
Big spoon
Tongs

STEP 6: During the last 30 minutes of simmering the vodka sauce, grill the seasoned chicken thighs over direct medium heat. Your cooking time will vary depending on the size of the chicken thighs but will generally run 10 to 15 minutes per side.

STEP 7: When the chicken is fully cooked, remove the skin and chop the thighs into bite-sized chunks, cutting around the bones. Coat and toss with the vodka sauce. Sprinkle with fresh parsley and Parmesan cheese and serve.

Since this is grilled chicken in a heavy cream sauce, we are forced into a Chardonnay. Three Sisters Vineyards Fat Boy White is a fun and very good selection.

Are you an apartment dweller and can't find a grill? Cook this masterpiece on the stovetop with a grilling pan. Buy boneless chicken thighs to make it easier. Heat your grilling pan over medium heat, and once it is hot, grill the thighs for 5 to 10 minutes on each side until done. Cooking times will vary depending on the size and type of chicken, but boneless chicken will cook more quickly. Cook the sauce as instructed.

COCONUT-CRUSTED MALIBU SHRIMP

Yield 2 to 4 servings, depending on shrimp size

Our Malibu shrimp recipe is versatile enough to be served as an appetizer, side dish, or even a main course. Although we prefer to use massive-sized colossal shrimp, you can create a coastline treat for any occasion by simply adjusting the cooking time to the size of the shrimp you choose to use.

STEP 1: To make the marinade, combine the rum, molasses, lime juice, garlic powder, cayenne pepper, and ground ginger in a mixing bowl.

STEP 2: Put the shrimp in a quart-sized ziplock bag and top with the marinade mixture. Squeeze the excess air out of the bag and make sure that the shrimp are evenly coated. Refrigerate for 30 to 60 minutes.

STEP 3: While the shrimp are marinating, prepare the 3 bowls to create the coconut crust. To the first bowl, add the flour. In the second bowl, beat together the egg and water. In the third bowl, combine the coconut flakes, panko bread crumbs, and salt.

STEP 4: Remove the shrimp from the ziplock bag after 30 to 60 minutes and discard the marinade. Holding the tail, dip a shrimp in the

INGREDIENTS

½ cup light Malibu rum

2 tablespoons molasses

2 tablespoons fresh lime juice

1 teaspoon garlic powder

½ teaspoon cayenne pepper

¼ teaspoon ground ginger

2 pounds large shrimp, peeled and deveined

½ cup flour

1 egg

2 tablespoons water

1 cup sweetened coconut flakes

½ cup panko bread crumbs

¼ teaspoon salt

EQUIPMENT

Grill

Mixing bowl

Quart-sized ziplock bag

3 small mixing bowls

Cookie sheet

Tongs

flour, followed by the egg, and coat with the coconut mixture. Place on a cookie sheet and repeat with the remaining shrimp.

STEP 5: Refrigerate the cookie sheet for 30 minutes to allow the crust to adhere to the shrimp.

STEP 6: Grill over medium-high heat for 3 to 4 minutes per side until the coconut is toasted and the shrimp are firm. Serve immediately.

A good pale ale will complement this dish nicely. You can stick with your favorite local brew or track down some Boulevard Double-Wide IPA from Kansas City.

Even paradise has the occasional rainy day, so feel free to give this recipe a try indoors by baking for 12 to 15 minutes at 400 degrees in a conventional oven or deep-frying for 2 to 3 minutes in vegetable oil heated to 350 degrees.

BLOODY MARY BURNT END CHILI

Yield 4 servings

Recovering after a long night at the local watering hole typically calls for one of two traditional morning cocktails: the mimosa or the bloody Mary. It's hard to believe that any self-respecting man would be caught hoisting a fruity concoction served in a flute, so for this head-pounding occasion the bloody Mary is our overwhelming beverage of choice.

Since the brown bottle flu has a tendency to sneak up on you at any given moment, we always keep a stash of our favorite bloody Mary mix in the back of the liquor cabinet. If you're anything like us, it only takes one morning cocktail before we're back on our "A" game. And just like clockwork, the mostly full bottle gets tossed into the fridge where it's forgotten and left to spoil.

Well, my friends, with this recipe you'll no longer have to pour those fallen soldiers down the drain a few weeks after they've served you well. Instead, we'll be offering them up to the barbecue gods as part of the manliest meal of all time—BURNT END CHILI!!!

For those of you living outside the Kansas City barbecue universe, burnt ends are the charred tips of a smoked brisket. We always have these guys lying around for just this occasion, but in case you don't, you can always hit up your local barbecue joint for a takeout order. If burnt ends are hard to come by in your area, then 2 pounds of smoked brisket cut into 1-inch chunks will work just the same.

INGREDIENTS

4 strips bacon

½ medium onion, chopped

2 cloves garlic, chopped

2 tablespoons chili powder

1 teaspoon cumin

1 teaspoon dried oregano

1 teaspoon coarsely ground black pepper

½ teaspoon cayenne pepper

1 bottle (32 ounces) spicy bloody Mary mix

1 tablespoon Dijon mustard

1 can (8 ounces) tomato paste

1 can (10 ounces) diced tomatoes

1 can (4 ounces) green chiles

2 pounds burnt ends or smoked brisket

1 can (28 ounces) baked beans

STEP 1: Place the bacon in a large stockpot and fry until crispy. Remove the bacon from the grease and have yourself a nice snack. You can include the bacon in the chili if you want, but what you're really after here is the flavorful grease.

STEP 2: In the bacon grease, sauté the onion and garlic until the onion is slightly golden brown and caramelized.

STEP 3: Add the chili powder, cumin, oregano, black pepper, and cayenne pepper to the skillet. Stir in the bloody Mary mix, mustard, tomato paste, diced tomatoes, and green chiles. Simmer this mixture for 15 minutes to allow the flavors to combine.

STEP 4: Add the burnt ends (or brisket) to the pot and reduce the heat to low.

STEP 5: Rinse and drain the beans and add to the pot.

STEP 6: Simmer for 6 to 8 hours, stirring occasionally. Serve just like you would your normal chili.

EQUIPMENT

Stockpot
Spatula
Can opener

Adjust the heat with the type of bloody Mary mix you use or the amount of cayenne pepper you add.

It's always about striking a good balance, and because chili is hearty, it's best to drink something light. Amber or pale ale is an excellent selection. For the connoisseur, Alaskan Amber is a great choice.

This can be made in a slow cooker. Complete steps 1 to 3 in a large skillet, and then combine all the ingredients in a large slow cooker. Simmer on medium heat for 6 to 8 hours, stirring occasionally,

---

Captain Morgan Pirate
Bones (page 131)

Burnt End Pizza
(page 176)

Kansas City Caviar
(page 77)

Pepper Jack Chile Burger (page 107)
with Sweet-Potato Fire Fries (page 85)

Steak-Wrapped Shrimp (page 73)
and Bacon Gorgonzola Twice-
Grilled Potatoes (page 58)

Bacon-Wrapped Asparagus Bundles
(page 64) and Honey Mustard Barbecue
Scallops (page 197)

Bacon Explosion (page 43) with Eggs

Back platter: Smoky Jalapeño
Cheese Squares (page 84)
and MOINK Balls (page 54)
Front platter: Olives Stuffed with
Bacon and Blue Cheese (page 63)
and Atomic Buffalo Turds (page 56)

GRILLED PORT PORTOBELLO MUSHROOMS

Yield 4 servings

This can be served as a side dish to complement one of your fancier creations—Grilled Chopped Chicken with Vodka Sauce, perhaps (page 141)—or as a main dish for a vegetarian friend. These aren't your average mushrooms. These bad boys get marinated with a delicious combination of port wine and mustard barbecue sauce.

STEP 1: Clean the mushrooms using a damp paper towel. Don't soak them in water because they will absorb water very quickly. Remove the stems and pat the caps dry.

STEP 2: Combine all remaining ingredients in a gallon-sized ziplock bag and shake well. Add the mushroom caps and coat evenly. Marinate for 30 to 60 minutes. Do not overmarinate as the mushrooms will soak up everything and become overpowering.

STEP 3: Cook the mushrooms over direct medium heat for 4 minutes per side until tender.

INGREDIENTS

4 large portobello mushrooms, 4 to 5 inches in diameter

½ cup mustard-based barbecue sauce

1 tablespoon ground black pepper

3 tablespoons Worcestershire sauce

1 tablespoon port wine

1 tablespoon Lawry's Seasoned Salt

EQUIPMENT

Grill

Gallon-sized ziplock bag

Cooking spray

Tongs

For an additional treat, use a spicy vinegar-based barbecue sauce in place of the mustard-based sauce. Slice up the leftover mushrooms to use on burgers!

RED WINE ITALIAN BEEF

INGREDIENTS

1 teaspoon dried basil

1 teaspoon dried oregano

1 teaspoon dried rosemary

1 teaspoon dried thyme

1 teaspoon dried marjoram

½ teaspoon garlic powder

½ teaspoon ground black pepper

1 5-pound chuck roast

1 jar (12 ounces) pepperoncini

1 medium white onion, minced

2 cups beef broth

1 cup dry red wine

French bread

Provolone cheese

EQUIPMENT

Grill or smoker

Small bowl

Aluminum pan

Hickory or other light wood

Aluminum foil

Yield 8 to 10 servings

We've all got that friend or family member who's constantly showing up to a party with their favorite blend of wine—boxed wine, that is. After drinking two of the five liters from a plastic cup, they head on their way, leaving their tapped cardboard box to add to your cellar. Instead of trashing that box of wine, we've got the perfect recipe to put some of it to good use.

STEP 1: Combine the basil, oregano, rosemary, thyme, marjoram, garlic powder, and black pepper in a small bowl to create a rub.

STEP 2: Place the roast in an aluminum pan and completely coat the rub mixture over the entire surface of the roast.

STEP 3: Drain the pepperoncini, pull off the stems, and add them to the pan around the roast.

STEP 4: Add the onion to the pan around the roast.

STEP 5: Pour the beef broth and red wine into the pan.

STEP 6: Smoke with hickory over indirect heat at 225 degrees for 4 hours. After 4 hours, tightly cover the pan with aluminum foil and continue cooking until the internal temperature of the roast reaches 200 degrees.

STEP 7: Remove the pan from the smoker. Using 2 forks, shred the beef and return it to the pan of juices.

STEP 8: Slice a loaf of French bread in half lengthwise and divide into 6-inch portions. Mound the shredded beef mixture on the open face of the bread and cover with a slice of provolone cheese.

STEP 9: Return the open-faced sandwich to the grill and heat until the bread warms and the cheese on top melts. Serve with a side of juice for dipping.

This recipe also works great by substituting your favorite beer in place of the wine.

CHAPTER 7

INTERNATIONAL BARBECUE

Do we really want to travel in hermetically sealed pope-mobiles through the rural provinces of France, Mexico and the Far East, eating only in Hard Rock Cafes and McDonald's? Or do we want to eat without fear, tearing into the local stew, the humble taqueria's mystery meat, the sincerely offered gift of a lightly grilled fish head? I know what I want. I want it all. I want to try everything once.

—Anthony Bourdain, *Kitchen Confidential: Adventures in the Culinary Underbelly*

Most barbecue cooks rely heavily on domestic recipes. Generally this makes sense as barbecue is certainly one of America's favorite pastimes. However, we don't limit ourselves to food that's traditionally American. Here, we're taking some of the great international cuisine from the Mediterranean, North Africa, Asia, and other locales and adapting it for some great-tasting international barbecue!

The foods of the world have a wide array of spices, herbs, oils, and other ingredients that create a unique challenge, but also unique flavor. Whether we cook in the smoker, on the grill, or over an open flame, we're going to take these world-renowned recipes and create sensational international barbecue that you can enjoy on a multitude of occasions.

Let's start with a word of warning. Many of these items are not normally found in everyday grocery stores (hence part of the challenge), so you might have to visit various ethnic or specialty markets to find some of these ingredients. Along with the challenge of cooking these recipes comes the reward of expanding your arsenal of barbecue recipes and knowledge about barbecue ingredients to a whole new level!

BARBECUED CHICKEN SOUVLAKI

Yield 4 servings

Often when you find souvlaki, whether on a street corner or in an upscale Greek restaurant, it is cooked and served on a skewer. It's also commonly served on pita bread, which is how we're approaching it here. We've added a vinegar-based barbecue sauce to increase the flavor and the tenderness of this world-famous food. Hint: Have some on hand after a late night of enjoying ouzo. It's one of our favorite absorbers of alcohol!

STEP 1: To make the marinade, combine the olive oil, lemon juice, red wine vinegar, garlic, oregano, black pepper, pepper flakes, thyme, and barbecue sauce in a medium bowl or gallon-sized ziplock bag and shake well.

STEP 2: Seed the bell pepper and cut into 1-inch strips. Slice the chicken into 1-inch strips. Place both the chicken and pepper strips in the marinade. Slice the red onion and place half of the slices in the marinade. Set the remaining onion aside for garnish. Marinate for a minimum of 8 hours or overnight in the refrigerator.

STEP 3: Heat the oven on warm or the lowest setting, 125 to 150 degrees. Place the empty grill basket on a grill over medium-high

INGREDIENTS

3 tablespoons olive oil

¼ cup fresh lemon juice

2 tablespoons red wine vinegar

3 cloves garlic, minced

1 teaspoon dried oregano

½ teaspoon ground black pepper

1 tablespoon red pepper flakes

1 teaspoon dried thyme

¼ cup favorite vinegar-based Carolina barbecue sauce

1 red bell pepper

1 pound boneless, skinless chicken breasts

1 red onion

4 to 6 pita breads

¼ cup tzatziki sauce

Iceberg lettuce (optional)

1 tomato, chopped (optional)

Fried bacon (optional)

EQUIPMENT

Grill

Medium bowl or gallon-
    sized ziplock bag

Knife

Grill basket

Cooking spray

Tongs

Serving bowl

heat. Coat with a thin layer of cooking spray and dump all the mari-nated chicken and vegetables in the grill basket. If you don't have a grill basket available, you can use a disposable slotted foil pan found at the grocery store. Mixing regularly, cook 8 to 10 minutes until the chicken is thoroughly cooked.

STEP 4: While the chicken is cooking, warm the pita breads in the oven for 1 to 2 minutes. This can be done on the top rack of your grill as well.

STEP 5: Remove the grill basket from the grill and dump everything into a serving bowl. Spoon into pita bread and add a tablespoon of tzatziki sauce. Garnish with fresh onion, lettuce, and tomato if you prefer.

If you want to make the tzatziki sauce yourself, blend the following until smooth in a food processor and refrigerate at least 1 hour: 2 (8 ounce) containers plain yogurt, 1 medium cucumber (peeled, seeded, and diced), 2 tablespoons olive oil, 3 cloves garlic, 2 tablespoons fresh dill, 2 teaspoons salt, and 1 teaspoon red wine vinegar.

The crisp bite and lemon flavor of Brooklyn Summer Ale pairs perfectly with this Greek dish. If you want to stick to the traditional, try Mythos Lager, which you should be able to find in specialty liquor stores. Don't forget the ouzo for a little after-dinner toasting.

FASSOULAKIA YAHNI (GREEK GREEN BEANS)

Yield 4 servings

No, we can't pronounce it either. Essentially this is the Greek version of green beans. This is a simple, easy-to-make Greek side dish that goes nicely with the Barbecued Chicken Souvlaki (page 153). It's a fairly standard side dish and pairs nicely with many different Mediterranean meals.

STEP 1: Heat the olive oil in a medium saucepan over medium heat. Add the garlic and onion and sauté until soft.

STEP 2: Add the chopped tomatoes and tomato paste. Bring to a boil and reduce the heat. Simmer until the sauce is slightly thickened, about 7 minutes.

STEP 3: Rinse the green beans in a colander with cool water and trim ¼ inch off the ends. Add the beans, chicken stock, and parsley to the sauce. If the beans are not fully immersed, add water until they are (it should not take much).

STEP 4: Cover and simmer until the beans are tender, about 30 minutes. Season with salt and pepper to taste. Serve immediately.

INGREDIENTS

1 tablespoon olive oil

2 tablespoons minced garlic

1 onion, chopped

1 can (14 ounces) chopped tomatoes

1 teaspoon tomato paste

1 pound green beans

1 can (14 ounces) chicken stock

2 tablespoons chopped fresh parsley

Kosher salt

Ground black pepper

EQUIPMENT

Medium saucepan

Spoon

GRILLED TANDOORI CHICKEN

INGREDIENTS

2 to 3 pounds boneless chicken breast or thigh

1 cup Greek yogurt (plain whole-milk yogurt will work if unavailable)

2 tablespoons fresh lemon juice

2 tablespoons cayenne pepper

2 teaspoons garam masala (a spice blend commonly found in large grocery stores or Asian specialty markets)

1 clove garlic, minced

1 teaspoon cayenne pepper

1 tablespoon paprika

2 teaspoons chopped fresh cilantro leaves

1 teaspoon salt

¼ teaspoon ground black pepper

1½ teaspoons coriander

1½ teaspoons cumin

1 teaspoon red food coloring

1 tablespoon unsalted butter, melted

Yield 4 servings

Marinated in yogurt, you ask? Don't let the yogurt fool you. It's a great blend of spicy chicken that is extremely popular in India and Pakistan. We love the unique spicy flavor of this chicken, and it's guaranteed to have you coming back for more. The recipe originated in British-controlled India and used a grill called a "tandoor," an egg-shaped grill made of clay. Many modern versions of tandoori dishes are cooked in the oven, but we're combining the oven and the grill to give you a multitude of options.

Tandoori chicken can be made from any part of the chicken, so cooking times will vary a bit. Don't be surprised at the color when it's done. It comes out red as a fiery dragon tongue!

Make sure you start early on this spicy specimen as it needs at least 8 hours of marinating time.

STEP 1: Remove all the skin and visible fat from the chicken. Cut into evenly sized portions and slice 2 or 3 ½-inch-deep cuts into each piece. This allows the marinade to penetrate deep into the chicken. Place in a gallon-sized ziplock bag or other suitable container.

STEP 2: Combine the yogurt, lemon juice, cayenne pepper, garam masala—actually, just combine everything but the butter, lime, and onion. Mix the ingredients until smooth (a blender or food processor makes this much easier). Pour three-quarters of the mixture into the ziplock and massage the marinade into the chicken. Reserve the remaining marinade for basting. Refrigerate the chicken for at least 8 hours (the longer the better in this case).

STEP 3: Preheat the oven (or a grill over indirect heat) to 400 degrees. Remove the chicken from the ziplock bag and discard the used marinade. Place the chicken in a glass baking dish, and just before placing the chicken in the oven, drizzle the melted butter over all. Basting frequently with the reserved marinade, cook for 30 minutes, turning the pieces over midway through cooking.

STEP 4: Remove the chicken from the baking dish and place it on a grill over direct medium heat for 8 to 10 minutes per side until the juices run clear. Serve with sliced lime and sliced onion and enjoy!

1 lime, sliced (optional)
1 onion, sliced

EQUIPMENT

Grill
Knife
Gallon-sized ziplock bag
Blender (optional)
Medium glass baking
    dish

A typical side dish is naan, a commonly found flatbread that is cooked along with items in the tandoor grill. It is served with almost all Indian food and is used to dampen the spice. To warm the naan, simply wrap it in foil and place it on the grill over direct heat for 5 to 10 minutes while grilling the chicken.

For those of you without access to a grill, tandoor or otherwise, this recipe is easily adapted to the oven. In step 3, preheat the oven to 450 degrees and place the chicken in a roasting pan. Cook approximately 30 minutes until the chicken is done and the juices run clear.

Although originally from England and made popular by the East India Trading Company, India Pale Ale is your beer of choice here. The hoppy combination blends well with the spicy Indian food.

To cut back on the heat, reduce the cayenne pepper to 1 tablespoon.

BARBECUED CHICKEN PAD THAI

INGREDIENTS

1 pound boneless,
  skinless chicken
  breasts

½ cup sweet barbecue
  sauce

2 tablespoons tamarind
  paste

¼ cup Asian fish sauce

¼ cup palm sugar (or
  unrefined dark
  brown sugar)

2 teaspoons minced
  garlic

1 teaspoon ground red
  pepper

½ teaspoon ground white
  pepper

1 package (14 ounces)
  thin Thai rice noodles

2 tablespoons vegetable
  oil

4 eggs (1 egg per serving)

¼ cup chopped green
  chives

½ cup chopped green
  onions

2 to 4 cups bean sprouts

½ lime, sliced

Sriracha chili sauce
  (optional)

Yield 2 servings

Pad Thai is one of the most popular dishes in Thailand and can be found on nearly every other street corner. That being said, just because it's served out of a vendor's cart doesn't mean it isn't some of the best food you'll get in Southeast Asia, or anywhere else for that matter. Toss in some barbecue chicken and a little smoke flavor to add to the mystique.

This recipe can be modified quite a bit to suit your taste. Don't like bean sprouts? Just leave them out. The best way to make this recipe is to just taste as you go; you're the chef so you get to eat first!

STEP 1: Place the chicken breasts in a ziplock bag with the barbecue sauce. Roll the chicken around so that each piece is evenly coated with sauce. Place in the refrigerator for 2 hours to marinate.

STEP 2: While the chicken is marinating, combine the tamarind, fish sauce, sugar, garlic, red pepper, white pepper, and barbecue sauce in a small bowl. Mix well and set aside.

STEP 3: Remove the chicken from the ziplock bag and discard any remaining marinade. Grill the chicken over medium direct heat for 5 to 7 minutes per side, or until the chicken is fully cooked. Remove the chicken from the grill, chop it into bite-size pieces, and set aside.

STEP 4: Fill a large bowl or pot with hot water. Soak the rice noodles in the water for 8 to 10 minutes. This will soften the noodles to the point where they are bendable but not quite soft enough to eat. Drain well and set aside.

STEP 5: Add 2 tablespoons vegetable oil to a preheated wok over high heat. Crack the eggs into the hot oil and begin stirring to break the yolks. Once the eggs begin to set, quickly add the noodles, sauce, chicken, chives, onion, and sprouts, stirring constantly to prevent clumping.

STEP 6: Cook, stirring constantly, for 1 to 2 minutes more, or until the noodles are soft. If the noodles absorb all the liquid and begin sticking to the wok before they are fully cooked, add 1 tablespoon water to rehydrate the pan.

STEP 7: Remove from the heat and serve immediately. Garnish each serving with a slice of lime and chili sauce to taste.

EQUIPMENT

Gallon-sized ziplock bag
Knife
Mixing bowls
Wok
Spatula

Tamarind and palm sugar may not be available in your local grocery store, but the majority of Asian specialty markets carry them. A good substitute for palm sugar is dark brown sugar and a bit of molasses. White vinegar can be substituted for the tamarind, although the flavor will be a little less sour and a bit more tangy. If green chives can't be found, simply omit.

A malty Belgian ale pairs perfectly with the spicy flavors found in this Thai dish. Duvel and Bison Belgian Ale are both commonly found across the country.

GRILLED KARNIYARIK (GRILLED SPLIT BELLY EGGPLANT)

INGREDIENTS

4 medium eggplants

Kosher salt

Olive oil

½ pound ground beef

2 large tomatoes

1 white onion

4 green banana peppers, seeds and stems removed, chopped

1 teaspoon ground cinnamon

1 tablespoon tomato paste

⅓ cup chopped fresh flat-leaf parsley, plus more for garnish

Ground black pepper

EQUIPMENT

Grill

Knife

Large bowl

Medium skillet

Grater

Spatula

Large skillet

Foil pan

Spoons

Grill grate (optional)

Yield 4 servings

Karniyarik is an interesting combination of rich flavors. Of Turkish origin, this is a widely popular dish as eggplant and other light vegetables often make up the meal during the hot summer months in Turkey. The majority of *karniyarik* recipes are made in the oven, but, of course, barbecue makes *karniyarik* better!

STEP 1: Remove the stem from the smaller end of the eggplant. Using a paring knife, remove a ½-inch strip of skin that starts from the cut end and runs down one side, underneath the large end, and back up the other side to the cut end. If done correctly, this slice would be a guideline to perfectly slice the eggplant in half lengthwise, although that's not what you're going to do.

STEP 2: Instead of slicing the eggplants in half, make a slice on one side to create the "split belly." To do this, hold the eggplant in one hand with one of the peeled edges facing upward. Using the paring knife, start 1 inch from the top end and carefully slice three-quarters of the way through the eggplant. Continue slicing the length of the side, stopping 1 inch from the bottom. As the eggplant softens, this slice will expand, creating an opening to fill with the stuffing.

STEP 3: To remove the bitter flavor that naturally occurs in eggplant, soak them in a bowl of water mixed with 2 tablespoons salt for 30 minutes.

STEP 4: Heat 1 teaspoon olive oil in a medium skillet. Add the ground beef and grate one of the tomatoes and the onion in as well. Grating the ingredients instead of chopping them gives the stuffing a more robust flavor since it will give you the juice as well. Using a spatula, combine the ingredients and begin to sauté over medium heat. Add the chopped peppers and ground cinnamon.

STEP 5: Sauté the mixture over medium heat until most of the liquid is absorbed. The beef doesn't have to be completely cooked yet, as it will be grilled later. At the very end, add the tomato paste, parsley, and salt and pepper to taste (approximately 1 teaspoon each to start). Cover and remove from the heat.

STEP 6: Remove the eggplants from the salt water and squeeze as much water as you can from them. Dry with paper towels.

STEP 7: Heat 1 teaspoon olive oil in a large skillet. Lightly brown the eggplants for approximately 4 minutes on all sides until soft.

STEP 8: Remove the eggplants from the skillet and place in a foil pan, slit side up. Using 2 spoons, open up the eggplants as much as possible without breaking them. Stuff as much of the filling as you can inside the eggplants. Depending on the size of the eggplants, this will come out to about 4 tablespoons each. Cut the second tomato into wedges and place on top of the eggplants. Now you're ready to grill.

STEP 9: Place the foil pan on a grill over medium direct heat and close the lid. Grill for approximately 30 minutes. After 20 minutes, check on them every 5 minutes for tenderness as you don't want them to get too mushy.

STEP 10: Remove the pan from the grill. Garnish with parsley and pour any additional sauce over the top. Serve and enjoy a fine grilled Turkish eggplant!

For a completely different texture, use a grill grate rather than the aluminum pan. You have to be an expert with your tongs or you'll lose your stuffing, so be extra careful! Grill until the outside is browned (15 to 20 minutes). Add cherry wood (page 10) for some smoke flavor that will give you something extra special!

Although traditional Turkish dishes are not accompanied by alcohol, we're still going to give our recommendation. Grab a Guinness Stout to complement the complex flavors of the eggplant. For wine lovers, reach for a Spanish wine called La Rioja Alta.

TANGY BARBECUE SHASHLIK

Yield 4 servings

Trying to track down the origins of shashlik is fruitless, as this form of cooking has been around since fire. Shashlik is a popular item found on street corners in Russia and Israel. This hearty food is traditionally cooked on a mangal grill (essentially a rectangular pit filled with hot coals) and marinated in very acidic juices. There are a multitude of regional variations, but in this recipe we're going with a Russian version, as we love the unique flavor.

STEP 1: Trim the fat from the lamb and cut the meat into 1-inch cubes. This step can take some time because lamb has quite a lot of fat on it. Cut the sirloin steak into 1-inch cubes.

STEP 2: Prepare the marinade in a bowl by combining the lemon juice, olive oil, black pepper, salt, paprika, cilantro, cayenne pepper, red wine, garlic, and red wine vinegar. Mix well.

STEP 3: Combine the cubed meat and marinade and place in a gallon-sized ziplock bag. Cover the meat throughout, seal, and refrigerate for 3 to 8 hours.

STEP 4: Cut the onions into eighths. Remove the seeds from the green peppers and cut into 1-inch squares.

INGREDIENTS

1 pound lamb loin chops
1 pound beef sirloin steak, boneless
½ cup fresh lemon juice
½ cup olive oil
1 teaspoon ground black pepper
1 teaspoon salt
1 teaspoon paprika
1 teaspoon chopped fresh cilantro
¼ teaspoon cayenne pepper
1 cup red wine
1 clove garlic, minced
2 tablespoons red wine vinegar
2 medium onions
2 large green bell peppers
12 ounces button mushrooms

EQUIPMENT

Knife
Medium bowl
Gallon-sized ziplock bag
Cooking spray
Metal skewers

STEP 5: Apply a light coat of cooking oil to metal skewers to make your feast easy to remove after cooking. Place the marinated beef, lamb, and mushrooms, onions, and green peppers on the skewers in whatever order floats your boat.

STEP 6: Place the skewers on a grill over direct medium-high heat for 3 to 4 minutes per side for medium-rare, or longer to desired doneness.

For crispier vegetables, create vegetable-only skewers and grill for just the last 5 minutes of cooking time. Basting all the skewers with barbecue sauce during the last 5 minutes is also a good option, since everything on earth is better with barbecue—sauce!

For a Russian dish, we recommend a fine bottle of vodka. Toast a few shots, chased with pickles. If you're going to drink beer, remember that the Russians think "drinking beer without vodka is simply spending money." But if you must, stick with their native Baltika-brand beer.

MEDITERRANEAN SHREDDED HALIBUT STEW

Yield 4 servings

This easy-to-make dish transforms a standard Mediterranean grilled fish recipe into a chunky stew rich with flavor.

STEP 1: Rinse the halibut and peel away any skin still on the fillet. Peeling the skin is similar to pulling the membrane on ribs. Occasionally you'll need a knife to trim the difficult parts. Rub the fish with Nantucket rub or your favorite seafood seasoning and set aside.

STEP 2: In a medium saucepan, add the olive oil, onion, tomatoes, whole olives, wine, basil, parsley, and garlic powder. Bring to a boil over high heat, then reduce the heat to medium and simmer for 6 minutes.

STEP 3: Grill over direct medium-low heat for 5 minutes per side until the fillet flakes easily with a fork.

STEP 4: Remove the fish from the grill. Shred into bite-sized pieces and divide equally among 4 bowls.

INGREDIENTS

1 pound firm halibut fillet

2 tablespoons favorite seafood rub

1 tablespoon olive oil

½ cup finely chopped onion

2 cans (12 ounces each) diced tomatoes

½ cup Kalamata olives, pitted

2 tablespoons white wine

2 teaspoons dried basil

2 teaspoons chopped fresh flat-leaf parsley

½ teaspoon garlic powder

Salt and pepper to taste

½ cup crumbled feta cheese

EQUIPMENT

Grill

Knife

Medium saucepan

Cooking spray

STEP 5: Spoon the sauce equally over the fish. Add salt and pepper to taste. Sprinkle feta cheese over the dish and serve!

If it's too cold out to grill (which it never is in our opinion) or you are stuck in your studio apartment, this dish can be easily made in your oven. Just preheat the oven to 425 degrees and bake the fish in a glass baking dish (use cooking spray) for 15 to 20 minutes until the fish flakes easily with a fork.

Any good Chardonnay or Riesling will pair nicely with this halibut stew.

AFRICAN PORK RIBS

Yield 4 to 6 servings

This recipe uses a hot paste called harissa that is a standard in North African cuisine. Fairly popular around the world, harissa paste and sauce is found everywhere north of the Sahara desert. Get your safari gear together and serve this unique pile of ribs at your next party.

STEP 1: Combine the harissa, lemon juice, garlic, coriander, and bird pepper in a small bowl and set aside.

STEP 2: Rinse and pat dry the ribs. Peel the membrane, using a butter knife as we explained on page 20, and trim the excess fat. You'll be shooting for an even width across the length of the rib.

STEP 3: Rub both sides of the ribs with salt and pepper and slather generously with your harissa sauce. Try to cover the ribs completely with the slather. Wrap in plastic wrap and refrigerate overnight.

STEP 4: Let the ribs sit for 30 minutes at room temperature before cooking. Place the ribs bone side down on a 225-degree smoker over indirect heat.

STEP 5: Baste the ribs gently with beer every 30 minutes, doing your best to keep the harissa sauce on the ribs. Cook until the ribs reach

INGREDIENTS

¾ cup harissa paste

3 tablespoons fresh lemon juice

1 tablespoon minced garlic

1 teaspoon crushed coriander seeds

1 teaspoon African bird pepper (or cayenne pepper)

2 or 3 racks baby back pork ribs

Kosher salt

Ground black pepper

1 16-ounce beer

EQUIPMENT

Grill or smoker

Small bowl

Basting brush

Tongs

Heavy-duty aluminum foil

an internal temperature of 140 degrees and the meat has started to pull away from the bones (approximately 2 hours).

STEP 6: Remove the ribs from the grill and individually wrap each slab in heavy-duty aluminum foil. Add 1 tablespoon beer to each foil packet before sealing tightly. Cook to an internal temperature of 200 degrees (approximately 2 more hours), or until the slabs pass the bend test (page 20). Remove from the smoker, slice, and serve.

Harissa paste can be found at Middle Eastern markets and Whole Foods.

If it's winter and you can't handle the cold, or if you're in a Manhattan high-rise and don't have a grill, you still have options. Heat the oven to 250 degrees and place the ribs on the middle rack. Place a foil pan or something similar on the lower rack to catch any drippings. Follow the above directions including all temperature readings and timings, and you're good to go.

For your beer selection, grab a six-pack of Sam Adams or Leinenkugel's. Both of these will complement the variety of spices in these ribs.

Spareribs can be substituted for baby back ribs, although they take a bit longer to cook (pages 18 to 20). Plan to smoke the spares an additional hour before wrapping in aluminum foil.

BRAZILIAN BEEF CAJUN CREOLE

Yield 6 servings

This fusion recipe combines the heat from a Brazilian style beef stew, barbecue, and Cajun food for a meal that is sure to light up your mouth.

STEP 1: Dice the onion and green pepper and mince the chiles (see step 4, page 77, for handling chiles). Cut the red potatoes into small chunks and chop the celery. Slice the andouille sausage into 1-inch rounds, flake the crab, and place both in a medium bowl. Set aside.

STEP 2: Cut the beef tenderloin into 1-inch cubes and set aside.

STEP 3: Mix the barbecue beef rub, thyme, oregano, basil, Cajun seasoning, and bay leaves in a small bowl.

STEP 4: Peel and devein the shrimp and remove the tails. In a medium pot, bring 2 quarts water to a boil and boil the shrimp for 3 minutes. Drain and set aside.

STEP 5: Using a grill basket, grill the beef and potatoes over direct medium heat for approximately 10 minutes, stirring regularly. If you do not have a grill basket, you can grill the beef and potatoes whole and slice them after.

INGREDIENTS

1 medium onion

1 green bell pepper

2 serrano chiles

2 medium red potatoes

2 ribs celery

½ pound andouille sausage, cooked

¼ cup lump crab meat, any shell pieces removed

1 pound beef tenderloin

1 tablespoon barbecue beef rub

1 teaspoon dried thyme

1 teaspoon dried oregano

1 teaspoon dried basil

1 teaspoon Cajun seasoning

2 dried bay leaves

¾ pound small shrimp

½ cup olive oil

1 can (12 ounces) diced tomatoes

1 can (14 ounces) beef stock

1 clove garlic, minced

½ teaspoon Tabasco sauce

Brown or white rice

Salt and pepper to taste

STEP 6: In a large skillet, heat ½ cup olive oil over high heat. Add the chopped and diced vegetables, andouille sausage, crab, potatoes, and beef to the skillet. Add the diced tomatoes, beef stock, and minced garlic. Add the Tabasco sauce and bring to a boil. Reduce the heat, cover, and simmer for 25 minutes. Remove from the heat and let rest for 10 minutes.

STEP 7: While you are simmering the stew, prepare the rice.

STEP 8: Season the stew with salt and pepper to taste and serve over rice.

Abita Purple Haze is one of our favorite Louisiana beers and easily found in many liquor stores.

CHAPTER 8

LEFTOVERS

Leftovers make you feel good twice. First, when you put it away, you feel thrifty and intelligent: "I'm saving food!" Then a month later when blue hair is growing out of the ham, and you throw it away, you feel really intelligent: "I'm saving my life!"

—George Carlin

Food is often just as good or better the second time around. This is especially true when you create a masterpiece meal using leftover barbecue. We know that there are rarely times when you actually *have* leftover barbecue, but that just gives you an excuse to make more the first time around!

Growing up, we were slapped from all sides with leftovers from our parents. It wasn't until the early college days when we had to choose between leftover pizza and even older leftover pizza that we began to appreciate what could actually be done with our uneaten food. We'd have a brisket pizza (page 176) any day of the week.

We think it's a sin to let any barbecue go to waste, so the use of any leftovers is imperative to keeping our souls intact. This chapter gives you the ammo to create wonderful meals after your backyard barbecue is complete. Once you fly through these, you'll find hundreds of your own ideas to add, and your place in leftover sainthood will be achieved!

PULLED PORK FRIED RICE

Yield 6 servings

The Chinese got it right when they created pork fried rice. That's why we're offering up our leftover pulled pork to make their classic dish even better.

STEP 1: In a small bowl, combine the soy sauce, molasses, mustard, garlic, and ginger and set aside.

STEP 2: Scramble the eggs over medium heat in a greased large skillet. Using a spatula, break the eggs into small pieces while cooking. Remove from the heat and set aside in a small bowl.

STEP 3: Add the vegetable oil to the skillet and heat over medium heat. Add the peas and carrots and cook until tender.

STEP 4: Add the pulled pork to the skillet and cook until warm.

STEP 5: Add the cooked rice to the skillet and fry for 1 to 2 minutes.

STEP 6: Stirring constantly, pour the sauce over the top of the rice mixture and cook for another 2 minutes.

INGREDIENTS

1 teaspoon soy sauce

1 teaspoon molasses

⅓ teaspoon ground mustard

¼ teaspoon ground garlic

⅓ teaspoon ground ginger

2 eggs, lightly beaten

1½ tablespoons vegetable oil

½ cup frozen green peas, thawed

½ cup frozen sliced carrots, thawed

2 cups pulled pork (page 25)

2 cups cold cooked rice

Salt and pepper to taste

EQUIPMENT

Small bowls

Large skillet

Cooking spray

Spatula

STEP 7: Remove from the heat and stir in the scrambled eggs. Season to taste with salt and pepper.

This recipe also works great with chicken or shrimp.

If you don't have any cooked barbecue meat on hand, you can fry raw protein in the oil before adding the vegetables to the skillet.

Since we're having fried rice, you can always stick with Tsingtao, the most commonly found beer in China. Or you might want to go with a light pale ale like Sierra Nevada or Boulevard Pale Ale from Kansas City since you'll be getting a lot of barbecue pork flavor.

SMOKED CHICKEN SALAD

Yield 4 servings

Anytime we fire up the cooker, we always try to make room for some extra chicken. It's quick and easy to cook, and the leftovers make a standard chicken salad even better.

STEP 1: In a medium bowl, combine the barbecue sauce and mayonnaise and whisk until smooth.

STEP 2: Add the chicken, celery, eggs, and green onions. Toss gently, coating all ingredients.

Although we like the added flavor of smoked chicken, feel free to use grilled or baked chicken in its place.

INGREDIENTS

¼ cup barbecue sauce

¼ cup mayonnaise

2 cups smoked chicken (page 33), diced

1 rib celery, diced

2 smoked (page 79) or hard-boiled eggs, diced

¼ cup chopped green onions, white and green parts

EQUIPMENT

Medium bowl

Knife

Whisk

BURNT END PIZZA

INGREDIENTS

1 tube pizza dough

1 tablespoon butter

½ Vidalia onion, sliced

2 cups burnt ends
  (page 29)

1 cup thick and spicy
  barbecue sauce,
  warmed

¾ cup shredded smoked
  Gouda

¾ cup shredded
  mozzarella

EQUIPMENT

Pizza pan

Sharp knife

Skillet

Yield 4 servings

Although we're hard pressed to have any of our burnt ends left over, we'll go out of our way to reserve some for this smoky pizza pie.

STEP 1: Preheat the oven to 400 degrees.

STEP 2: Prepare the pizza dough according to the instructions on the tube.

STEP 3: Melt the butter in a skillet over medium heat. Add the onion and sauté until translucent. Add the burnt ends and heat until warm.

STEP 4: Spread the barbecue sauce evenly over the pizza crust and top with the warm burnt ends and onion. Evenly cover the entire pizza with cheese.

STEP 5: Bake for 10 to 15 minutes until the cheese is bubbly.

If burnt ends are hard to come by in your area, then sliced, chopped, or cubed brisket will work just as well.

Pizza and beer. You can't go wrong with a pitcher of your favorite domestic light beer. Bud Light or Miller Lite, we can never agree.

CAROLINA-STYLE PULLED PORK SPRING ROLLS

INGREDIENTS

1 pound pulled pork
    (page 25)

¼ cup chopped onion

2 cloves garlic, minced

1 jalapeño pepper, finely
    diced

2 cups shredded green
    cabbage

¼ cup shredded carrots

2 tablespoons barbecue
    sauce

1 tablespoon flour

1 tablespoon water

1 package wontons or
    egg roll wrappers

Vegetable oil

Barbecue rub

SLAW-STYLE DIPPING SAUCE

½ cup mayonnaise

1 tablespoon vegetable
    oil

1½ tablespoons sugar

1 teaspoon white vinegar

¼ teaspoon celery seeds

⅛ teaspoon salt

Yield 16 servings

Pulled pork and coleslaw are a perfect marriage. Wrap them both up in dough and toss them in a deep fryer. Now you're talking fantasy!

STEP 1: Warm the pulled pork, onion, garlic, and jalapeño in a large skillet over medium heat for approximately 5 minutes.

STEP 2: Stirring constantly, add the cabbage and carrots to the skillet and fry for about 3 minutes until the cabbage becomes tender. Remove from the heat and stir in the barbecue sauce.

STEP 3: In a small bowl, mix the flour and water to form a paste. This will be the glue that holds the spring roll together while frying.

STEP 4: Place 1 wonton wrapper on a work surface with a corner facing toward you and top with ⅓ cup of the cabbage mixture.

STEP 5: Fold the front corner of the wonton over the cabbage mixture. Repeat for the left and right corners.

STEP 6: Brush the edges of the remaining wonton with the flour paste and tightly fold the last edge over the top of the roll.

STEP 7: Before frying the spring rolls, prepare the dipping sauces. In 2 separate bowls, mix all the ingredients together and set aside.

STEP 8: Heat vegetable oil in a deep fryer to 375 degrees. Deep-fry 2 or 3 spring rolls at a time for 1 to 2 minutes until golden brown. Remove to paper towels to drain briefly. Season with barbecue rub and serve immediately with both dipping sauces.

Tsingtao for the spring roll, and Carolina Blonde for the pork. You'll just have to drink both at the same time!

SPICY BARBECUE DIPPING SAUCE

¼ cup barbecue sauce
¼ cup white vinegar
1 teaspoon hot sauce

EQUIPMENT

Large skillet
Spatula
Mixing bowls
Deep fryer
Tongs

BARBECUE GRINDERS

INGREDIENTS

Unsliced sesame seed deli
    rolls
Barbecue sauce, warmed
Barbecue meat, warmed
Shredded mozzarella
    cheese
Olive oil
Barbecue rub

EQUIPMENT

Sharp knife
Basting brush
Aluminum foil

Grinders are a Kansas City creation, so it's only fitting that we include our own barbecue version.

STEP 1: Preheat the oven to 350 degrees.

STEP 2: Cut each deli roll in half widthwise and hollow out both sides of the bread.

STEP 3: Coat the inside of the bread with a thick layer of warm barbecue sauce.

STEP 4: Alternate layers of 1 tablespoon meat and 1 tablespoon cheese until the bread is full. Top with a final layer of cheese.

STEP 5: Lightly brush the outside of the bread with olive oil and sprinkle with barbecue rub.

STEP 6: Wrap tightly in aluminum foil and bake for 15 minutes. Serve with a side of barbecue sauce.

To honor the original grinder, try using smoked sausage and marinara.

Another Kansas City creation deserves a Kansas City beer. Grab any specialty brew from Boulevard and you'll be set. Try out one of the seasonal beers if you can find it. Bob's '47 Oktoberfest lands at the top of our list.

BRISKET BIEROCKS

INGREDIENTS

2 teaspoons butter

1 cup chopped onion

1½ pounds smoked brisket (page 29), chopped

4 cups chopped cabbage

2 tubes crusty French loaf bread dough

1 egg

2 tablespoons water

EQUIPMENT

Large skillet

Spatula

Sharp knife

Baking sheet

Spoon

Small bowl

Basting brush

Yield 16 bierocks

Let's face it . . . Hot Pockets suck. The real reason we eat them is because they're quick and convenient. The next time you think about purchasing a Costco-sized case, try making up a batch of these brisket bierocks instead. They're a traditional German meat-filled pastry that's made even better with leftover smoked brisket.

STEP 1: Preheat the oven to 350 degrees.

STEP 2: Melt the butter in a large skillet over medium heat. Add the onion and sauté until translucent. Add the brisket and cabbage and cook until the cabbage is tender. Remove from the heat and drain any liquid that may have gathered.

STEP 3: Unwrap a tube of bread dough and unroll. Cut the dough into 4 equal-sized squares, then cut each square diagonally in half. Repeat for the other tube.

STEP 4: Spoon an equal amount of the brisket mixture in the center of each triangle. Wrap the 3 corners of the triangle around the brisket mixture and pinch the corners together on top to seal the mixture inside and place on a baking sheet.

STEP 5: Combine the egg and water in a small bowl with a fork and use a basting brush to thinly apply egg wash on the top of each bierock.

STEP 6: Bake for about 30 minutes until the bread is crispy. Let cool for 5 minutes before serving.

The world is your oyster when selecting a beer for this. You may have already had several so just pick your favorite. Anything is good with barbecue bierock!

SEARED TOMATO BRISKETTA

INGREDIENTS

1 French baguette

6 Roma tomatoes, halved

Olive oil

10 smoked brisket slices (page 29), halved, warmed

1 cup crumbled goat cheese

Fresh basil leaves

EQUIPMENT

Grill

Tongs

Sharp knife

Yield 6 servings

Brisketta is our barbecue infused version of the classic Italian bruschetta. The creamy goat cheese complements the smoky brisket and the slight sweetness of the seared tomato. These are best served as appetizers while your main course is still cooking.

STEP 1: Cut the baguette into ¾-inch-thick slices. Grill over direct high heat for 1 to 2 minutes per side until browned.

STEP 2: Place the tomato halves cut side down on the grill and sear for 2 to 3 minutes until grill marks have formed.

STEP 3: Lightly drizzle the baguette slices with olive oil and rub the seared tomato halves on the toasted surface of the bread to leave a tomato smear.

STEP 4: Top with 2 to 3 slices of warm brisket and a sprinkling of goat cheese. Garnish with fresh basil and serve immediately.

PULLED CHICKEN AND MUSHROOM FAJITAS

Yield 8 fajitas

This recipe is a great leftover meal that you can prepare in advance or just before you're ready to eat. We like to take these foil-wrapped bundles and put them directly on the firebox of our smokers. They heat up in no time and always give us the much needed energy boost to push through the next twelve hours of competition cooking.

STEP 1: In a medium bowl, combine the chili powder, oregano, paprika, and garlic powder. Pull the smoked chicken or pork into bite-sized strips and coat evenly in the spice mixture.

STEP 2: Heat the oil in a medium skillet over medium heat. Add the onion, mushrooms, and bell peppers and sauté until the onion is translucent.

STEP 3: Lay out the tortillas and spread an equal amount of chicken, mushroom mixture, tomatoes, salsa, and cheese on each one. Roll and wrap tightly in foil.

STEP 4: Preheat the grill to medium-high. Place the fajitas on the grill and cook on each side for about 5 minutes. Serve with additional salsa if desired.

INGREDIENTS

1 tablespoon chili powder
½ teaspoon dried oregano
½ teaspoon paprika
¼ teaspoon garlic powder
1 pound smoked chicken (page 33) or pulled pork (page 25)
2 tablespoons olive oil
1 small onion, sliced
2 cups sliced button mushrooms
1 green bell pepper, sliced
8 large flour tortillas
2 medium tomatoes, diced
Salsa of choice
½ cup shredded Cheddar cheese

EQUIPMENT

Grill
Medium bowl
Sharp knife
Medium skillet
Aluminum foil

This recipe also works great as a breakfast dish. Prepared early, it's perfect for those camping trip mornings. Simply substitute 8 scrambled eggs, chopped ham, and breakfast potatoes for the mushrooms, onion, pepper, and chicken. Cook as directed.

This recipe can also be baked in a 400-degree oven for 15 minutes.

Any amber ale goes well with spicy food and barbecue, so this is the obvious choice here. Try Green Flash Hop Head Red Ale and you won't be disappointed.

CHAPTER 9

WIVES, GIRLFRIENDS, AND MISTRESSES

If there hadn't been women we'd still be squatting in a cave eating raw meat, because we made civilization in order to impress our girlfriends. And they tolerated it and let us go ahead and play with our toys.

—Orson Welles

We don't want to stereotype here; we love the ladies that like barbecue sauce all over their faces. Traditionally, however, the grill has been the man's domain. Ladies, it's time to make it your own and show us Neanderthals how it's done! And guys, don't worry at all, this chapter will help you out in more ways than one.

Ladies, if you want to impress your man, there's no better way than to bust out some barbecue and let him know you mean business. Besides, when we say we like tofu burgers and artichoke hearts, who are we kidding? And don't think it just has to be a pile of beef smothered in barbecue sauce. Serve him up some smoked prime rib, and he'll be under your spell for as long as you wish!

Gentlemen, if you want to impress your date with a fancy dinner but don't want to lose all of your man points, then we've got you covered. Fire up the grill and prepare a fine dinner of Honey Mustard Barbecue Scallops with a side of Spinach Artichoke Oysters on the Half Shell and she'll wonder how she ever got so lucky!

Finally, foremost on everyone's mind when that meet-the-parents moment comes is what to do for dinner. Any and all recipes in this chapter have you covered from all sides. You still get to grill for Dad. You still get to serve something fancy for Mom. And, most important, you still get to barbecue.

SPINACH ARTICHOKE OYSTERS ON THE HALF SHELL

Yield 12 oysters

Whether you're preparing appetizers for a roomful of guests or setting the mood for that special someone, these are a surefire winner. You can even double the spinach artichoke filling for a quick and easy dip.

STEP 1: Heat the butter in a medium skillet over medium heat. Add the garlic and sauté for 3 to 4 minutes.

STEP 2: Add the spinach and sauté until wilted but still bright green. Remove the pan from the heat, add the cream cheese, and stir until combined.

STEP 3: Add the artichoke hearts and all but ¼ cup of the cheeses. Stir to combine.

STEP 4: Place a spoonful of the dip on top of each shell, completely covering the oyster.

STEP 5: Top with a pinch of the remaining cheese and a light sprinkling of paprika.

INGREDIENTS

1 teaspoon butter

2 cloves garlic, minced

2½ cups shredded fresh baby spinach

6 ounces cream cheese, at room temperature

1 can (14 ounces) artichoke hearts, drained and chopped

⅔ cup shredded Fontina cheese

⅔ cup grated Asiago cheese

⅔ cup grated Parmesan cheese

Salt and pepper to taste

12 large oysters on the half shell

Paprika

EQUIPMENT

Grill

Medium skillet

Spatula

Spoon

STEP 6: Grill over direct medium-high heat until the cheese is bubbly. Let cool for 5 minutes before serving.

An excellent choice to complement oysters is Blackstone Winery Pinot Grigio. It's commonly found at grocery stores and liquor stores throughout the country and is a high-quality wine for the price.

SMOKED PRIME RIB

Yield 10 to 12 servings

If you are unsure of your cooking abilities, prime rib can be an intimidating meat to prepare because of its price. Luckily, prime rib is a relatively simple dish, and it's made even better with the addition of a rich smoky flavor. Keeping in mind the high cost of this cut of meat, we HIGHLY recommend using some sort of temperature probe (page 14) to monitor the internal temperature of the meat. A few degrees can make a big difference when dealing with prime rib.

STEP 1: In a small bowl, combine the brown mustard and steak sauce to form a thin paste. Slather the rib roast with the mixture, coating the entire cut of meat.

STEP 2: In another small bowl, combine all the dry ingredients to create a rub.

STEP 3: Apply a heavy coat of rub over the entire surface of the rib roast.

STEP 4: Smoke at 250 degrees over indirect heat until the internal temperature reaches 135 degrees. This should take 4 to 5 hours, but you should be monitoring the internal temperature instead of watching the clock.

INGREDIENTS

1 tablespoon brown mustard

1 tablespoon steak sauce

1 8 to 10-pound prime rib roast

2 teaspoons kosher salt

2 teaspoons ground black pepper

2 teaspoons garlic powder

2 teaspoons cayenne pepper

2 teaspoons chili powder

2 teaspoons paprika

HORSERADISH CREAM SAUCE

½ cup sour cream

3 tablespoons mayonnaise

3 tablespoons prepared horseradish

1 tablespoon apple cider vinegar

2 teaspoons Dijon mustard

1 teaspoon salt

EQUIPMENT

Smoker or grill

Small bowls

Aluminum foil

STEP 5: Remove the roast from the grill and immediately wrap in aluminum foil to contain the juices. Let sit for 30 minutes.

STEP 6: Mix the ingredients for the cream sauce together in a bowl.

STEP 7: Slice the roast and serve with the sauce.

A medium-bodied red wine like Shiraz is the perfect complement for smoked prime rib. Four Sisters Shiraz is one of our picks.

DOUBLE HOT TUNA STEAKS

Yield 6 servings

This recipe takes advantage of the two kinds of heat that the culinary world has to offer. Wasabi provides a quick sinus heat that fades into the more familiar pepper heat of the chili sauce. Neither are over-powering, and they're both complemented by the sweet ginger flavor that comes from the marinade.

STEP 1: In a mixing bowl, combine the soy sauce, maple syrup, hot sauce, ginger, garlic, and lemon juice.

STEP 2: Place the tuna steaks in a large ziplock bag and cover with the marinade. Let marinate in the refrigerator for 2 to 4 hours, flipping hourly.

STEP 3: Remove the steaks from the marinade. Coat each side with ¼ teaspoon wasabi and immediately coat with the ground wasabi peas. (If the wasabi paste is too thick to spread on the steaks, dilute it with a splash of soy sauce.)

STEP 4: On a well-oiled grill, sear the steaks over direct high heat for 2 to 3 minutes per side. This will create a rare to medium-rare tuna steak, which is what you are shooting for. Buying high-quality tuna

INGREDIENTS

1 cup soy sauce

¼ cup pure maple syrup

1 tablespoon hot sauce

¼ teaspoon ground ginger

¼ teaspoon garlic powder

1 teaspoon fresh lemon juice

6 tuna steaks (6 to 8 ounces each, about 1 inch thick)

CRUST

3 teaspoons prepared wasabi

½ cup hot wasabi peas, finely ground in a food processor

Salt and pepper

EQUIPMENT

Grill

Mixing bowl

Large ziplock bag

Tongs

is in your best interest. Season with salt and pepper and serve immediately.

If wasabi peas are hard to come by in your area, you can substitute panko bread crumbs.

The combination of spicy wasabi and tuna is a unique combination calling for a unique wine. Try a Chenin Blanc, typically bottled in California or France.

HONEY-BRINED SAVORY CHICKEN BREASTS

Yield 4 servings

These chicken breasts have been a staple on our grill for years. They're versatile enough to be served as plain fillets, sandwich style, or even a salad topper.

STEP 1: Place the chicken breasts on a cutting board. Using the flat side of a meat tenderizer (or the bottom of a small pan), pound each chicken breast until it's a uniform thickness of about ½ inch throughout the entire cut.

STEP 2: Combine the water, salt, honey, rosemary, and thyme in a gallon-sized ziplock bag. Seal completely and shake vigorously until all the salt is dissolved, creating brine.

STEP 3: Place the chicken breasts in the bag and make sure they are fully submerged in the solution. Refrigerate for 1 hour.

STEP 4: Remove the chicken from the brine, pat dry, and season with black pepper to your liking.

STEP 5: Grill over direct medium heat for 8 to 10 minutes per side until the internal temperature reaches 165 degrees or until the juices

INGREDIENTS

4 boneless, skinless
    chicken breast halves
2 cups water
2 tablespoons kosher salt
2 tablespoons honey
¼ teaspoon dried
    rosemary
¼ teaspoon dried thyme
Pepper
4 slices pepper Jack
    cheese

EQUIPMENT

Grill
Meat tenderizer
Gallon-sized ziplock bag
Tongs

run clear when the breast is poked with a fork. During the last 2 minutes of cooking, top each chicken breast with a slice of pepper Jack cheese.

To make this chicken recipe into a delicious sandwich, place a cooked fillet on a bun with lettuce, tomatoes, and a 50/50 mixture of barbecue sauce and Baconnaise.

This smooth chicken dish should be served with a smooth beer to complement it. Try Chimay Blue, brewed by Trappist monks since 1862. Don't worry—you can usually find it locally.

HONEY MUSTARD BARBECUE SCALLOPS

Yield 6 to 8 servings

INGREDIENTS

½ cup honey mustard

½ cup Kansas City–style barbecue sauce

1 tablespoon minced garlic

1 tablespoon chopped fresh parsley

1½ pounds sea scallops

EQUIPMENT

Grill

Medium bowl

Whisk

Gallon-size ziplock bag

Cooking spray

Tongs

Scallops are one of those recipes that seem to be the same in just about every cookbook on the planet. The only thing missing is the sweet taste of Kansas City barbecue.

STEP 1: Combine the honey mustard, barbecue sauce, garlic, and parsley in a medium bowl and whisk until blended.

STEP 2: Place the scallops in a gallon-sized ziplock bag and pour in half of the marinade. Coat the scallops evenly and refrigerate for at least 2 hours.

STEP 3: Grill the scallops over direct medium heat for 3 to 4 minutes on both sides until the outside is browned and the center is opaque.

STEP 4: Serve with the remaining marinade drizzled on top.

You can mix up the flavor every time you cook this recipe by changing the type of barbecue sauce you use. A hot North Carolina sauce will completely change everything. Try a variety of sauces and find the one you like best!

Select a Chardonnay or Riesling for white wine drinkers. If you prefer red, stick with Merlot.

PEPPER-CRUSTED BLUE CHEESE FILETS

Yield 4 servings

INGREDIENTS

4 filet mignon steaks (6 ounces each)
2 tablespoons coarsely ground black pepper
1 tablespoon kosher salt
8 ounces blue cheese

EQUIPMENT

Grill
Cooking spray
Tongs

Sometimes we're amazed how something so simple can be so good. But when simple involves filet mignon and blue cheese, it's an obvious no-brainer. This four-ingredient recipe is not only quick and easy, it will give you the big, bold flavor found in famous chophouses around the country.

STEP 1: Season the steaks on both sides with a thick coating of pepper and kosher salt.

STEP 2: Create a two-zone cooking surface by setting up your grill to have direct high heat on one side and direct medium-low heat on the other.

STEP 3: Sear the steaks over direct high heat for 2 minutes per side.

STEP 4: Move the steaks over to the medium-low side and cook for an additional 6 to 8 minutes until the steak is cooked to your liking.

STEP 5: During the last 2 minutes of cooking, top each steak with 2 ounces of blue cheese and close the lid on the grill.

STEP 6: Remove the steaks from the grill and let them rest for 5 minutes before serving.

Stick with a dry red wine like Merlot or Cabernet Sauvignon. The blue cheese factors in here, so leaning toward a fruitier wine is ideal.

CHAPTER 10

DESSERTS

Seize the moment. Remember all those women on the Titanic who waved off the dessert cart.

—Erma Bombeck

Desserts aren't something you would normally equate with barbecue, but that certainly doesn't mean you can't have any. Although we tend toward pulled pork and bacon for dessert, there are a myriad of delicious options you can create to satisfy a sweet tooth.

A common misconception is that you can't make any decent dessert on a grill or smoker. Well, we certainly beg to differ as do the hundreds of competition barbecue teams that create mouthwatering desserts every year. With a few tricks up your sleeve, you'll be doing the same thing in your own backyard!

After finishing off that rack of ribs, two pulled pork sandwiches, some burnt ends, and a slice of Bacon Explosion, who wouldn't want a nice big portion of Hobo Monkey Bread? Whatever you decide to make for dessert, it's guaranteed to seal your fate into total food coma!

HOBO MONKEY BREAD

This recipe adapts classic monkey bread to the grill in a unique way. This technique also works great next to a campfire.

STEP 1: Using cooking spray, lightly grease the inside of each empty soup can.

STEP 2: In a large ziplock bag, combine the white sugar and cinnamon. Shake to blend.

STEP 3: Using kitchen shears or a bread knife, cut each biscuit into 4 equal-sized portions.

STEP 4: Place 8 biscuit pieces into the ziplock bag and evenly coat with the sugar mixture. Evenly distribute the coated pieces among the cans. Repeat for the remaining pieces.

STEP 5: In a small saucepan over direct medium heat, combine the butter and brown sugar, stirring constantly. Just before the mixture boils, remove it from the heat and pour into the cans, distributing it equally among all 6.

INGREDIENTS

½ cup white sugar

1 teaspoon ground cinnamon

2 tubes buttermilk biscuits

½ cup butter

1 cup brown sugar

EQUIPMENT

Smoker or grill

Cooking spray

6 empty vegetable or soup cans (15-ounce size)

Large ziplock bag

Kitchen shears or bread knife

Small saucepan

STEP 6: Using a small portion of wood chips, lightly smoke the monkey bread over indirect heat at 300 degrees for 30 to 45 minutes until the biscuits have risen and are no longer doughy.

STEP 7: Let cool for 5 to 10 minutes and enjoy straight out of the can.

If needed, rotate the cans halfway through to promote even cooking.

Try adding walnuts and/or raisins to your Hobo Monkey Bread.

GRILLED CANDY BARS

INGREDIENTS

8 teaspoons
    Marshmallow Fluff
4 small flour tortillas
4 candy bars
4 teaspoons unsalted
    butter, melted
Sugar

EQUIPMENT

Smoker or grill
Aluminum foil
Tongs

Candy bar preferences are as regional as barbecue flavors. Luckily no matter if you're a fan of Whatchamacallit or an Almond Joy loyalist, this recipe is sure to satisfy your sweet tooth.

STEP 1: Spread 2 teaspoons Marshmallow Fluff on each tortilla and place a candy bar in the center of each tortilla.

STEP 2: Wrap the tortilla around each candy bar, completely sealing it inside with the Marshmallow Fluff.

STEP 3: Brush the outside of the tortillas with melted butter and sprinkle lightly with sugar. Wrap each one tightly in aluminum foil.

STEP 4: Grill over medium heat for 5 minutes on each side until the candy bar is melted. Cool for 2 to 3 minutes before unwrapping the foil and serving.

These are great on camping trips too. Prep the candy bars in foil packets before you leave and place in a cooler. Once the campfire is going, place the foil wraps near the fire and heat until the candy bar has melted.

CANDIED PINEAPPLE STICKS

INGREDIENTS

1 pineapple, peeled and
   cored
½ cup pure maple syrup
¼ cup dark brown sugar
Cayenne pepper to taste

EQUIPMENT

Smoker or grill
Metal skewers

Seared fruit is one of our favorite desserts to prepare on the grill. A caramelized sugar crust is the best way to make nature's candy even bettter.

STEP 1: Standing the pineapple on end, cut in half lengthwise. Repeat this process until you have 8 uniform pineapple spears.

STEP 2: Insert a metal skewer lengthwise into each pineapple spear and brush with maple syrup. Liberally sprinkle with brown sugar and cayenne pepper.

STEP 3: Grill over medium heat for 5 to 10 minutes per side until the sugars caramelize. Cool for 2 to 3 minutes before serving.

CHOCOLATE CRÈME BRÛLÉE

Yield 6 servings

Hello!!! You get to use a propane torch! Anything you do that allows you to play with fire is a good idea, especially when it results in an absolutely delicious chocolate dessert. And did we mention you get to use a torch?

STEP 1: Preheat the oven to 350 degrees.

STEP 2: To separate the eggs, crack an egg on a flat surface near the middle of the egg. Over a small bowl, crack the shell into 2 pieces, letting the yolk settle into the lower half while the egg white drains into the bowl. Transfer the yolk back and forth between the eggshell halves until the egg white has drained off and place the yolk in a large bowl. The fast and messy way to separate them is to crack the egg into your hand and let the white drain through your fingers. Whisk the egg yolks until smooth and set aside.

STEP 3: Add the cream, vanilla, 1 cup sugar, and Kahlúa to a microwave-safe glass bowl. Stir until the sugar is blended and add the milk chocolate, chocolate chips, and cocoa powder. Heat in a microwave oven on 50% power for approximately 2 minutes until the chocolate is soft. Remove and whisk until smooth.

INGREDIENTS

9 large eggs, separated

4 cups heavy cream

½ tablespoon vanilla extract

1 cup sugar, plus 6 tablespoons for sprinkling

1 ounce Kahlúa

1 ounce milk chocolate

¼ cup semisweet chocolate chips

2 ounces cocoa powder

EQUIPMENT

Large bowl

Whisk

Microwave-safe glass bowl

6 ramekins (8 ounces each)

Large baking pan

Culinary torch

STEP 4: Slowly pour the chocolate mixture into the egg yolks while whisking. Divide the chocolate mixture among the 6 ramekins.

STEP 5: Place the ramekins in a large baking pan and fill the pan with hot water until water reaches halfway up the ramekins.

STEP 6: Bake until the center of the crème barely jiggles when the pan is shaken gently, 25 to 35 minutes depending on your oven. Remove the ramekins from the water and let cool completely. You can cool them in the refrigerator; just be careful of the hot ramekins. Refrigerate for at least 2 hours.

STEP 7: When you are ready to serve, remove the ramekins from the refrigerator and dust each one evenly with 1 tablespoon sugar. Break out your torch to caramelize the top. To do this successfully, you'll want to use a lot of movement and go in spurts. Don't let the flame hit the sugar directly as it will be too heavily scorched. Let the ramekins sit for 5 minutes and serve.

Clearly not everyone has a culinary torch. If you don't, go get one because frankly they're just fun to play with. You can easily use any type of torch with odorless gas (a BernzOmatic propane torch for example). If for some reason you can't go out and get one, you can caramelize in the oven. Preheat the broiler and place the ramekins on the top rack closest to the heat. Broil for 2 to 3 minutes until the sugar bubbles and turns a light brown. Pay close attention because they can burn quickly!

KANSAS CITY GOOEY BUTTER CAKE

Yield 12 servings

This is called Kansas City Gooey Butter Cake because . . . well, we made it in Kansas City. Based loosely on the original version which originated in St. Louis, this cake has an interesting history. Legend has it that it was created when a St. Louis baker accidentally reversed the proportions of sugar and flour. Good thing he faltered because this is one of our favorite desserts.

STEP 1: Preheat the oven to 350 degrees.

STEP 2: In a large bowl, combine 1 cup of the flour, 3 tablespoons of the sugar, and 3 tablespoons cocoa powder. Using a hand mixer on low speed, blend in $\frac{1}{3}$ cup ($5\frac{1}{3}$ tablespoons) butter until the mixture is crumbly. If you're without a hand mixer, you can use 2 forks just as easily. Pat into the bottom of a 9-inch square baking pan.

STEP 3: In a large bowl, combine $2\frac{1}{2}$ cups sugar, the cream cheese, almond extract, $\frac{3}{4}$ cup (12 tablespoons) butter, and the egg. Beat with the mixer until combined.

STEP 4: Beat in 1 cup flour and the evaporated milk alternately and continue to beat until combined but still lumpy. Pour into the crust-

INGREDIENTS

2 cups all-purpose flour

2½ cups white sugar, plus 3 tablespoons

3 tablespoons cocoa powder

1$\frac{83}{100}$ cups unsalted butter (just kidding—that's ⅓ cup plus ¾ cup total)

¾ cup cream cheese, at room temperature

2 teaspoons almond extract

1 large egg

⅔ cup evaporated milk

Powdered sugar (optional)

EQUIPMENT

2 large bowls

Handheld mixer

9-inch square baking pan

lined pan. Bake for 35 minutes until the cake is nearly firm when you shake it.

STEP 5: Let the cake cool. Cut into servings and sift powdered sugar over the top.

We're not really sure who actually invented this recipe. In reality there are at least five different versions of the story, as well as several families also taking credit for it. We don't really care because it's just full of gooey, crumbly goodness.

STRAWBERRY RHUBARB CRUMB CAKE

Yield 12 servings

This dessert is specially made to be put on the grill immediately after removing your meat. Let it cook while you enjoy dinner, and it will be done just as you're ready for dessert!

STEP 1: Spray 13 x 9-inch grill-safe baking dish with cooking spray. Combine the sugar, salt, 1 cup of the flour, the oats, cinnamon, egg, milk, vanilla, and nutmeg in a mixing bowl. Cut ½ cup (8 tablespoons) of the butter into small pieces and add to the mixing bowl. Using a handheld mixer on low speed, blend in the butter until all is crumbly and well blended. Spread the cake batter evenly in the baking dish.

STEP 2: Wash and hull the strawberries and slice. Wash the rhubarb and cut into ½-inch pieces, discarding the ends. Top the batter with the strawberries and rhubarb.

STEP 3: Create the topping by combining the brown sugar, remaining ½ cup flour, and remaining ½ cup (8 tablespoons) of butter. Using a fork, mix until well combined and the mixture begins to form clumps. Refrigerate until ready for use.

INGREDIENTS

1 cup sugar

¼ teaspoon salt

1½ cups flour

½ cup rolled oats

½ teaspoon ground cinnamon

1 large egg

⅔ cup milk

1 teaspoon vanilla extract

¼ teaspoon ground nutmeg

1 cup (16 tablespoons) butter, at room temperature

3 cups strawberries

2 cups rhubarb

1 cup (packed) brown sugar

EQUIPMENT

Grill

13 x 9-inch grill-safe baking dish

Cooking spray

Medium mixing bowl

Handheld mixer

Aluminum foil

STEP 4: Preheat a grill to medium, around 350 degrees. If you've just finished cooking, cover the baking dish with foil and place it on the grill so it can bake while you enjoy your dinner. Cook for 20 minutes and remove the foil. Top evenly with the crumb topping and cook for an additional 15 to 20 minutes until the top is golden brown. Let cool for 30 minutes before serving.

This can be easily baked in the oven. Skip the foil and cook in the oven for the same time, at the same temperature, and following the same directions.

GRILLED S'MORES

Yield As many as you want

INGREDIENTS

Graham crackers
Hershey bars
Marshmallows

EQUIPMENT

Grill
Aluminum foil

Who says you can't have s'mores when you're not camping? You could potentially call this cheating since it's so easy.

STEP 1: Preheat a charcoal or gas grill to low. Build the s'more by layering 1 graham cracker square, 1 chocolate square, and 1 marshmallow and topping it off with another graham cracker.

STEP 2: Loosely wrap each serving in foil and seal at the top. Place on the middle or top rack of the grill and cook for 4 to 5 minutes on low until everything melts into a gooey chocolate surprise.

STEP 3: Go get some paper towels and eat. Repeat. Each packet makes one delicious s'more.

You can also make these in a 225-degree oven. Place them on a cookie sheet and bake for 3 to 5 minutes. That said—if you're cooking s'mores in the oven, maybe you should get out s'more.

JASON'S ACKNOWLEDGMENTS

Writing this book has truly been a labor of love. Barbecue is a deep passion of mine, and writing this book has been an experience of a lifetime. There are countless people who made this project possible, so I apologize if I don't mention you all.

Thank you to Lisa Grubka, Beth Wareham, Whitney Frick, and Scribner for seeing our vision and taking a chance on two meatatarian bloggers from Kansas City. Your efforts and support have made this possible.

My beautiful wife, Megan, for all your love and support while I chase my dream. You've been right there with me every step of the way and this book is a direct result of your love and encouragement.

My parents, siblings, grandparents, aunts, uncles, cousins, and in-laws for your willingness to offer up your taste buds and opinions. Family is a big part of my life, and each one of you is constantly contributing to my world of food. I sincerely thank you for that.

My friends and fellow Burnt Finger BBQ teammates, Bryant Gish and Aaron Chronister. Our common passion for barbecue is what started this crazy ride.

And last but not least, a special thanks to Rodney and Cecilia Dyche of All American BBQ for their help in the early days of Burnt Finger BBQ. You guys truly embody the spirit of competition barbecue.

AARON'S ACKNOWLEDGMENTS

A large number of people contributed in helping us make this book what it is today. First I'd like to thank my wonderful wife, Jenny, for her infinite patience with all of my barbecue equipment that is scattered around the house and in the driveway and for her help with a lot of the cooking and experimenting in this book. I couldn't have done it without you.

I would like to thank our editor, Beth Wareham, for fixing the hundreds of grammatical errors I made while writing this book (including these acknowledgments), and all her great ideas during the whole process. Thanks to Whitney Frick and all the people behind the scenes at Scribner for their hard work and support. Thanks to our agent, Lisa Grubka, for working so hard on our behalf and her patience in dealing with us on our first book.

The birth of this book came from a perfect storm of events. I would like to say thank you to Rae Hoffman for threatening to inflict bodily harm upon me if I didn't start a barbecue website. I'd like to thank my partner, Jason, for coming up with the idea of the Bacon Explosion in the first place and for doing the majority of the work on this book. Thanks to Bryant Gish, the other member of our competition team; without his help none of this could have happened. Thanks to our friends Rodney and Cecilia Dyche of All American BBQ for their invaluable mentoring during all of our competitions; we hope to see you holding more first-place trophies! Also thanks to Todd Johns of Plowboys BBQ for your help and advice; I know you'll be hoisting more first-place trophies for a long time.

Specifically Bacon Explosion related, I'd like to give special thanks to Jim Scott. Without his selfless and relentless help, we would never have been able to even begin creating any products. I'd also like to thank Chris Marks of Ace of Hearts BBQ for following us around the country on our first media tour and having a Good-One Smoker ready and waiting when we needed it. Jeff Stehney of Oklahoma Joe's BBQ shared his endless knowledge and helped get the Bacon Explosion off the ground here in Kansas City.

Finally, I'd like to thank all of you who contributed to this book in any way. There are too many to mention but we know and will remember the significant help you provided.

APPENDIX

Starting Your Library

One of the best things you can do to speed up the learning curve of barbecue is to study what others have done before you and learn from their trials and tribulations. There are plenty of great books about this style of cooking and each can provide a different perspective on how to master it. We have an extensive library of barbecue books that we're constantly expanding, but these are the ones we consider to be our go-to guides:

- *Paul Kirk's Championship BBQ,* Paul Kirk
- *Backyard BBQ,* Richard McPeake
- *Peace, Love, and Barbecue,* Mike Mills and Amy Mills Tunnicliffe
- *Dr. BBQ's Big-Time Barbecue Cookbook,* Ray Lampe
- *The Barbecue! Bible,* Steven Raichlen

Online Resources

The Internet has opened up the floodgates on what was once a secret-recipe-driven society. While elements of secrecy still exist within the barbecue community, there are plenty of online resources where you can ask questions, share ideas, and socialize with fellow pitmasters who are willing to divulge their techniques. Although BBQAddicts.com is our home, we regularly venture out to explore other great resources that the Internet has to offer.

- www.bbq-brethren.com: Easily the world's largest online barbecue community, where you can interact with all levels of barbecue enthusiasts from around the world.

- www.virtualweberbullet.com: The one-stop shop for anything and everything related to the best-selling smoker in the world, the Weber Smoky Mountain. This site is packed full of articles, videos, and discussion forums to get you up and running in no time flat.
- www.amazingribs.com: The tips and tricks mecca for smoking ribs.
- www.thepickledpig.com: Run by a fellow KCBS competition team, this Web site is a great resource for anything to do with competition barbecue. These guys openly share their award-winning recipes and are one of the few teams that post pictures of their competition turn-in boxes. In addition, their site also tracks competition results for every team competing on the KCBS circuit.
- www.KCBS.us: With more than ten thousand members worldwide, the Kansas City Barbecue Society is the world's largest organization of barbecue and grilling enthusiasts. They sanction more than three hundred barbecue contests across the country, publish a monthly magazine, and serve as a clearinghouse for all things barbecue.

One of our favorite concepts to come from the Internet is the blog. In case you're unfamiliar with this term, a blog is an online journal or diary where a person, or group of people, publicly posts articles about their work, family, hobby, or any particular subject that happens to interest them. Since trial and error is a big part of mastering the art of barbecue, it's no surprise that there's plenty of blogs out there documenting people's experiences with various degrees of success. While each one can contain some form of useful (or entertaining) information, here's a list of barbecue bloggers that have a long track record of churning out quality posts:

- www.thebbqgrail.com
- blog.smokeindaeye.com
- www.livefireonline.com
- divaqbbq.blogspot.com
- www.plowboysbbq.com
- pelletenvy.blogspot.com
- whitetrashbbq.blogspot.com
- www.ulikafoodblog.com

If there's one thing this world doesn't have enough of, it's barbecue radio shows. Even here in Kansas City, the barbecue capital of the world, we lack a quality radio program that's dedicated to the art of outdoor cooking. Luckily, the Internet can tap you directly into radio stations and podcasts from around the world to satisfy your listening needs. There's only one show that we listen to religiously, and we're confident you'll enjoy it as much as we do:

- www.thebbqcentral.com: Hosted by Greg Rempe, the BBQ Central Show is a weekly radio program that airs every Tuesday at 9:00 PM EST. His Web site also contains an archive of past shows in case you happen to miss one, or just want to relive one of the past discussions.

Not only are we addicted to barbecue, but we also have an insatiable appetite for bacon. Recently, these fried strips of pork belly have become quite trendy and newsworthy, so various Web sites have popped up to keep track of the happenings surrounding the bacon industry. Here are a few of our go-to sources for up-to-date bacon info:

- www.mrbaconpants.com: One of our favorite bacon blogs that also streams a live TV show on their home page. Although bacon is their main focus, they'll also throw in the occasional beer review for good measure.
- www.blueribbonbaconfestival.com: The home of the premiere bacon festival in the world.
- www.baconunwrapped.com: Bacon aficionado and published author Heather Lauer provides glimpses into her bacon-centered world.
- www.bacontoday.com: This Web site's tagline says it all: "Daily Updates on the World of Sweet, Sweet Bacon."

World-Class Competitions

In the world of competition barbecue, three major contests reign supreme. While there are countless events throughout the year, hearing your name called at the awards ceremony of these three contests is the highest honor a pitmaster can receive. Each of these contests does a great job of providing entertainment for the general public. So even if you're not competing, you can still have a fantastic time.

- www.arbbq.com: The American Royal Barbecue is the largest barbecue contest in the world. Located in Kansas City, the first weekend in October, it hosts both an invitational and open contest in which more than five hundred teams go head-to-head with hopes of being crowned the king of barbecue.
- www.jackdaniels.com: The Jack Daniel's World Championship Invitational is considered by many to be the most prestigious contest on the circuit. Not only do you have to win a grand championship to be eligible to cook "The Jack," but your name must also be pulled during a raffle-style selection process before you're invited to compete. Pitmasters will wait their entire lives to cook this contest, and yet some will never even get the chance.
- www.memphisinmay.org: The Memphis in May World Championship is a pork lover's dream. This contest focuses solely on swine, as cooks enter their best ribs, shoulder, or whole hog with hopes of taking home one of the biggest prize purses on the circuit.

Commercial Smokers and Grills

Deciding which smoker or grill to purchase can be a daunting task. Many different makes and models are available, so it's best to do your research and determine which type of cooker will best suit your needs before making the big purchase. To help you out, we've created a list of our favorites.

- www.weber.com: There's a reason why Weber is the most-recognized company in the barbecue industry. They manufacture numerous models of smokers and grills to fit everyone's needs. Their Smoky Mountain cooker is considered by many to be the highest-quality smoker that won't break the bank.
- www.aceofheartsbbq.com: Ace of Hearts BBQ is home to one of our favorite cookers, the Good-One line of grills and smokers. We own a few different versions of their cookers and even use them during competition.

- www.americanbbqsystems.com: Traditional style meets modern technology with these electronic rotisserie smokers.
- www.backwoods-smoker.com: This is quickly becoming one of the most coveted smokers on the competition trail; cooks using these insulated cookers have won every major title that the competitive barbecue world has to offer.
- www.spicewineironworks.com: Another great line of insulated smokers. If you have specific needs, they'll even help you design a one-of-a-kind custom cooker.
- www.biggreenegg.com: The industry-leading kamado-style cooker sports thick ceramic walls for fuel-efficient grilling and smoking. The Big Green Egg's ability to sustain high temperatures also makes it great for baking pizza and bread.
- www.bubbakeg.com: This steel kamado-style cooker offers the same great features as its ceramic counterpart at a reduced price. Built for mobility, the Bubba Keg comes with a built-in trailer hitch mount so you can haul it anywhere you need to cook.
- www.traegergrills.com: Pellet-based grills that make barbecuing as simple as setting an oven.
- www.cookshack.com: The home of the original electric smoker. They have various makes and models, some of which are banned from competition because of their automated-cooking process.

To access the members-only area of BBQAddicts.com, please use this password: 8FYDLFS3.

INDEX

Page numbers in *italics* refer to illustrations.

cheese(y) (cont.)
    Swiss, in Reuben/Rachel fatty,
        116–17
    see also blue cheese; Cheddar
        cheese; Mozzarella cheese
cheeseburger fatty, bacon,
    122–23
Chenin Blanc, 194
cherry wood, for smokers, 10
chicken, 31–32
    barbecue, pad Thai, 158–59
    breasts, honey-brined savory,
        195–96
    burger, blue cheese buffalo,
        101–2
    cuts of, 31–32, 31
    grilled chopped, with vodka
        sauce, 141–42
    grilled tandoori, 156–57
    Jamaican rum and coke,
        135–36
    pulled, and mushroom fajitas,
        185–86
    simple barbecue, 33–34
    souvlaki, BBQ, 153–54
    whole, cooking time, 16
chicken salad, smoked, 175
chicken stock, in fassoulakia yahni
    (Greek green beans), 155
chile burger, pepper Jack,
    107–8
chili, bloody Mary burnt end,
    145–46
Chimay Blue, 196
chips, grilled Asiago cheese,
    88–89
chocolate crème brûlée, 207–8
Christmas Day: breakfast fatty,
    126
Chronion, 4

Chronister, Aaron 2, 3–4
chuck roast, in spicy Italian beef,
    148–49
Clavin, Cliff, 129
clean up, for tailgates, 72
CNN, 6
Coca-Cola, in Jamaican rum and
    coke chicken, 135–36
coconut-crusted Malibu shrimp,
    143–44
collagen, converted into gelatin,
    17
competitions, barbecue, 221–22
cooking times, 16
corn, in Kansas City caviar,
    77–78
corn bread, smoky bacon,
    60–61
corned beef, ground, in Reuben/
    Rachel fatty, 116–17
Corona, 57
crab:
    cake-stuffed mushrooms,
        80–81
    meat, in Brazilian beef Cajun
        Creole, 169–70
cream, heavy:
    in chocolate crème brûlée,
        207–8
    in grilled chopped chicken
        with vodka sauce, 141–42
cream cheese:
    in atomic buffalo turds,
        56–57
    in creamy mushroom steak-
        burger, 99–100
    in Kansas City gooey butter
        cake, 209–10
    in spinach artichoke oysters
        on the half shell, 189–90

creamy mushroom steakburger,
    99–100
crème brûlée, chocolate, 207–8
crumb cake, strawberry rhubarb,
    211–12
crust, french-fried-onion, bacon
    mac and cheese with,
    67–68

Day, Jason, 1–3, 2
Dead Guy Ale, 76
December, 25, Christmas Day:
    breakfast fatty, 126
Des Moines, Iowa, Blue Ribbon
    Bacon Festival in, 42
desserts, 201–13
    candied pineapple sticks, 206
    chocolate crème brûlée,
        207–8
    grilled candy bars, 205
    grilled s'mores, 213
    hobo monkey bread, 203–4
    Kansas City gooey butter
        cake, 209–10
    strawberry rhubarb crumb
        cake, 211–12
deviled eggs, smoked, 79
Digg, 6–7
dipping sauce, for crab cake-
    stuffed mushrooms, 80–81
divaqbbq.blogspot.com, 220
Dos Equis, 57
Dr. BBQ's Big-Time BBQ Book
    (Lampe), 219
Duvel ale, 159

Easter: Scotch egg fatty, 121
egg(s):
    in bacon explosion breakfast
        casserole, 50–51

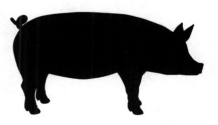